Priesthood and Ministry

Ecumenical Research

by

MAX THURIAN
Brother of Taizé

Translated by Paula Clifford

MOWBRAY
LONDON & OXFORD

Copyright © Presses de Taizé, 1970, 1983

ISBN 0-264-66920-7

Originally published 1970 in French as *Sacerdoce et Ministère*

First published in English language 1983
by A.R. Mowbray & Co. Ltd,
Saint Thomas House, Becket Street,
Oxford OX1 1SJ

Printed in Great Britain by Redwood Burn Ltd.

CONTENTS

INTRODUCTION

We are seeing at the present time a re-examination of certain forms of the Catholic presbyteral priesthood and the Protestant pastoral ministry. Admittedly the vast majority of priests and pastors are quietly adapting their ministry to the new demands of modern society and to changes in the Church. However, an important and active minority are challenging a clerical position which, they maintain, risks separating the minister from today's world and Christian people.

This challenge, which will undoubtedly turn into a fruitful dialogue for the future, may have considerable ecumenical significance; it may give us the chance to rethink together the distinctive character of evangelical ministry and to find again the common foundations of our doctrines, which have often been opposed on this point. This is not to simplify problems for the sake of a unity which would be too easy. To mention just two aspects of our traditional divisions, it must be remembered that the Protestant conception of ministry is less sacramental than that of the Catholic Church and that the Catholic idea of priesthood is more sacrificial; the Reformed tradition has developed a democratic synodical conception of the Church and ministry, while Catholic tradition has always retained a doctrine of the priesthood which is contained within an episcopal hierarchical order. But present tensions surely suggest that what has seemed irreconcilable in these theological positions may find an ecumenical solution in peaceful dialogue and in a healthy return to sources.

A heathly return to sources. It is worth dwelling a little on this point. There have indeed been Christians in history, and today as well, who, from a desire to return to the apostolic sources of the Church, seek to find the ideal life and ministry of the Christian community in the fervent Church of Corinth, at the time when St Paul was writing to it; a community of the Spirit, charismatically rich, where there was no explicit hierarchical and ministerial structure, even though it must be remembered that the apostle was exercising absolute authority from a distance. This type of return to sources, which is more biblicizing than biblical, is neither healthy or realistic. First, there is an evolution in the idea of the Church and ministry in the apostolic age. The New Testament also tells us about the Church and about the ministry of Timothy and Titus; and St. Ignatius of Antioch's idea of the episcopate at the dawn of the second century does not seem at the time to have appeared contradictory to the teaching of the apostles. Secondly, a return to sources does not mean the slavish imitation of a situation in the past. There is at times a contradiction between a desire to belong to the modern world and a wholly unrealistic return to sources.

A healthy return to sources consists in renewing from within, through biblical testimony, the concrete situations forged by centuries of uninterrupted tradition. We have inherited ideas of the priest or pastor which it would be unrealistic to reject just to jump back through time to the apostolic age, under the pretext of returning to sources, and thereby seeing the priest or pastor of tomorrow in an uncertain perspective. Christ who blessed the ministry at Corinth, Ephesus and Antioch, in the fourth century, the Middle Ages and the nineteenth century, however diverse its forms, is able to make today's ministry fruitful. It is not a case of replacing it *ex nihilo* by something completely new, but of renewing it in its authenticity by the force of God's word and by heeding the demands of modern society.

In studying scriptural passages about ministry it would be pointless to try to go back to an original conception beyond the text given to us by the New Testament writers. These first witnesses to the truth have recorded the facts for us, intermingled with their own interpretation of them, in the light of Christ's resurrection and by the power of the Holy Spirit, and placed them in the doctrinal and sacramental life and fellowship of the infant Church. What can enlighten us, in seeking a doctrine of ministry, is not the facts such as a journalist would have reported them but the testimony of men living in the resurrection of Christ and in the work of the Spirit in the Church. In the theological situation they passed on to us the truth of Christ, the Spirit and the Church, by which they lived, with much more authenticity and depth than if they had attempted the work of chroniclers.

Moreover, it is not possible to approach the facts and interpretations recorded in the New Testament without attempting to understand how the Church has received them into its life and tradition. Led by the Holy Spirit in the course of its history the Church does not cease to deepen its understanding of the Word of God. Scriptural accounts of the early Church can only be read as a living tradition, nourished by the life of Christ and the Spirit, and, in the light of the interpretation continually given to it by the Church in the course of its tradition, a perpetual deepening of the Gospel.

This renewal of the ministry through the sources of God's word and this adapting to contemporary conditions reveal fundamental precepts which are to be found throughout the living tradition of the Church, led by the Spirit. It is in these fundamental aspects that the special nature of ministry in the midst of God's people may be discerned and, today more than ever, the unity of the ideas of the Catholic priesthood and the Protestant pastorate, despite the differences which we have already stressed. We shall try to pinpoint the special nature of the ministry.

It is essentially the idea of ambassadorship in the name of Christ with the aim of reconciliation with God that defines the nature and function of ministry. St Paul writes: 'We are ambassadors for Christ, God making his appeal through us. We beseech you on behalf of Christ, be reconciled to God' (2 Cor. 5.20). The whole tradition bears witness to this fundamental notion. This ambassadorship is to serve the royal priesthood of all believers, to develop it and in turn put it to the service of mankind. However the ministry may have adapted to contemporary conditions, however immersed in the world's social conditions it may be, however 'declericalized', it can only be an apostolic ministry if it exercises this ambassadorship which indicates the verticality of the action of God, and the transcendence of his world. The selection of the priest or pastor may be hierarchical (Catholic) or more democratic (Protestant), but he will always be a believer set aside, not separated, ordained, not 'clericalized', as the ambassador of God among his brothers, to enable them to grow in their priesthood of the believers.

We see this ambassadorship at work in various basic functions that make up the ministry.

It is firstly the proclamation of the Word of God, contained in the Bible and lived out in the living tradition of the Church. This proclamation could take very new and different forms, but it will always be the news of the reconciliation of man and God through Christ who died and came to life again. The pastor will be able to enter into men's lives, he will be able to work like them and with them, he may be a teacher or labourer, but he will only really fulfil his ministerial function if he has in some way the possibility and the desire to proclaim the Gospel of Christ.

The pastor is also the man of sacrament and prayer. Through the celebration of the Eucharist he makes heard the action of grace of the people of God and he feeds them with the Body of Christ. Admittedly prayer is characteristic of every Christian, but the pastor is charged with a particular prayer of intercession. As a priest he brings before God the needs and concerns of those who are entrusted to him.

Finally, the pastor has an authority which is given to him by God, 'it is as if God was exhorting through him'. This authority is certainly not domination but a service to the Christian community to keep it in the unity of charity.

If ministry lacks any one of these elements it breaks down and loses its distinctive characteristic. If God's word is not proclaimed the ministry risks disintegrating into an optimistic and unrealistic human fraternalism. Without sacraments and prayer it admits a secularization of the Christian community which would soon become no more than a society for good works. Unless authority is exercised and accepted as serving unity in charity there is the likelihood of anarchy, division and vain arguments among Christians, which would be a scandal to the world which could no longer say, as in the early days of the Church: 'See how they love one another'.

We may rejoice in the enthusiasm of some in trying to renew the forms of ministry but it is important to remember the fundamental elements constituting its distinctive function and its faithfulness, without which it risks disintegrating into a worldly laicism. All the time Christian unity could be achieved in the mutual recognition of our ministries, once the truths of faith concerning them have been explored more deeply, it would be very sad if both sides were to lose the sound doctrine of ministry which we have in common. Our responsibility to the world, which expects the reconciliation of the Gospel, means that we must hold fast to that doctrine, throughout all the necessary and desirable changes.

First of all we shall go back to the source of all ministry: the priesthood of Christ. Next we shall see how the apostles lived out their ministry and gave it shape. Then we shall tackle the problem of ministries today: how, in the light of God's Word, should the Church understand the episcopate, presbyterate and diaconate both today and in the near future? Finally we shall study the problem of ordination to the ministry, the solution to which could mean the end of divisions and herald a new church life for Christians in a restored unity.[1]

(1) An outline of this study may be found in *Le pain unique* (Les Presses de Taizé, 1967): some elements have been taken from this book, which is now out of print.

PART ONE

THE PRIESTHOOD
OF CHRIST

1

THE MEDIATION OF THE SERVANT

Christ is the one high priest at the head of the Church, to transmit to men the salvation accomplished on the cross, to intercede with the Father that they might be sanctified by the Spirit and to lead them to eternal life in his kingdom. The Epistle to the Hebrews frequently expresses this unique priesthood of Christ, who completes the succession of the priesthood of the Old Covenant.[1] Having perfectly fulfilled his priestly ministry through the sacrifices of the cross, Christ remains for ever the one high priest: 'He holds his priesthood permanently, because he continues for ever. Consequently he is able for all time to save those who draw near to God through him, since he always lives to make intercession for them. For it was fitting that we should have such a high priest, holy, blameless, unstained... We have such a high priest, one who is seated at the right hand of the throne of the Majesty in heaven, a minister in the sanctuary and the true tent which is set up not by man but by the Lord' (Heb. 7.24–26; 8.1–2). The whole Church is a royal priesthood (1 Pet. 2.9) only because it takes part, as a body, in the activity of Christ, its head, in the world. The Church, the body of Christ, is the sign and instrument of the unique priesthood of Christ, for the salvation of mankind.[2]

The one high priest, at the head of the universal priesthood of believers, to bring about the redemption of the world, Christ is also the one pastor or bishop of the Church, to strengthen it in faith, to sanctify it through the sacraments and to govern it in unity: 'You were straying like sheep, but have now returned to the Shepherd and Gaurdian of your

9

souls' (1 Pet. 2.25). The only ministry given to the ministers
of the Church is that of Christ, 'the great shepherd of the
sheep, by the blood of the eternal covenant' (Heb. 13.20),
that is by the sacrifice of the cross. The ministers of the
Church share in the unique diaconate of Christ, who said
'Let... the leader [among you become] as one who serves... I
am among you as one who serves' (*diakonôn*, Luke 22.26–27);
the ministers of the Church share in the unique pastorate or
episcopate of Christ. They are the signs and instruments of
his ministry in order to build up the Church.[3]

It is from the basis of a doctrine of participation, of sign
and instrument, that we shall understand the nature and
meaning of ministry in the Church in the service of the royal
priesthood of all believers. It is therefore first of all necessary
to understand the priesthood and ministry of Christ. The
universal priesthood of God's people in the world and the
ministry of bishops, pastors and deacons in the Church are,
by virtue of participation, the signs and instruments of that
unique priesthood and perfect ministry of the Lord.[4]

Because of the wedge driven between man and God by sin,
in the face of man's inability to remove it despite all the voices
of the prophets, the Father sent his Son who became
incarnate by the Holy Spirit, taking a bodily form similar to
our own. Through the incarnation God indeed became man
to lead among us a truly human existence and thus to be to us
a perfect example. God became man in Jesus Christ to reveal
to us what man is, how to live and to love God and all men.

Christ therefore put himself totally in the place of man to
bring about his redemption. Christ did not come to meet
man, who might have been able to raise himself a little, to
help him along the rest of the path to him. Christ did not
come to bring man the strength he might need to rise out of
his lowly state to communion with God. Christ took man's
place to live completely a human life, in order that our
definitive redemption might be accomplished in that perfect
human life. It is through the communion of our weak, sinful
humanity with the perfect, holy humanity of Christ that we
are led into a movement which tears us from ourselves and
raises us up towards the Father. Christ, the incarnate Son of
God, lived as a man to tear us out of sin and out of ourselves,
to dwell in us through the Holy Spirit and to lead us into his
love and his obedience to the Father.[5]

Thus our salvation works through Christ's assuming our own humanity. 'I have been crucified with Christ', wrote St Paul, 'it is no longer I who live, but Christ who lives in me; and the life I now live in the flesh I live by faith in the Son of God, who loved me and gave himself for me' (Gal. 2.20). The man who, in faith, accepts Christ as his only saviour, as God himself who loved him and gave himself for him, continues of course to live as a man, in the flesh, and keeps his own unique personality; but Christ's presence dwells in him, leading him to crucify anything in him which separates him from God. He lives as a man, but Christ dwells in him, his existence radiates his presence, to bind him to God in a love which saves him from sin and from himself.

Christ, in his incarnation, descended to the depths of human misery to lead man into his obedience as a servant and into his glory as Lord. St Paul describes this descent of the Son of God to the depths of human misery and his raising up into God's glory, by exhorting us: 'Have this mind among themselves which is yours in Christ Jesus' (Phil. 2.5–11). The Son who shared God's glory did not take advantage of that unique rank which made him equal to the Father. He became as nothing, he entered into the misery of our humanity, made himself a servant by becoming like us in every respect except sin. His behaviour was truly that of a man, sharing all our humanity in all its weakness, agony and suffering. Much more, his humility, obedience and service took him to the tragic end of our human life: bodily death; and it was not the death of some happy, secure man, but the ignominious death of a criminal, abandoned by most of his friends, death by the terrible torture of the cross. He knew the depth of human misery when he voiced his anguish in the cry, 'My God, why hast thou forsaken me?'.

Because Jesus sank to this abasement through which he entered into full communion with that part of humanity furthest removed from God, every man can see himself in him and know that wherever he may be in the darkness of this world, however deep he may fall into human distress, Christ is with him to put himself in his place, to cry out with him in his loneliness, to live his poor life, to lead him into the movement of being raised up towards the Father, to breathe new life into him and hide his life with him in God.[6]

It is in this perspective of the incarnation of the Son, his total participation in our humanity, his taking the place of man to lead him out of misery into glory, that the priesthood of Christ must be understood: it is unique, it alone is possible, for only that sacrifice can reconcile us with God and restore us to perfect communion with him. Human priesthood and the priesthood of the Old Testament could not bring us peace with God, for the priests of this earth are subject to the same weaknesses as other men. Christ alone, the 'holy, blameless, unstained high priest' (Heb. 7.26), was able to offer the perfect and definitive sacrifice acceptable to God, and thus to win us redemption. He entered the heavenly sanctuary to offer the Father the memorial of the sacrifice of the cross and so become for us a living intercesson (Heb. 7.24–28).

It was at the time of his baptism by John in the river Jordan that Jesus was designated and consecrated the servant of Yahweh. Christ's baptism is a messianic consecration. The Holy Spirit came upon him to designate him God's Messiah. The Father's voice was heard: 'This is my beloved Son, with whom I am well pleased' (Mat. 3.17). Jesus was ordained as a servant of Yahweh, as foretold by the prophet Isaiah:

> 'Behold, my servant whom I have chosen,
>> my beloved with whom my soul is well pleased.
> I will put my Spirit upon him,
>> and he shall proclaim justice to the Gentiles.
> He will not wrangle or cry aloud,
>> nor will any one hear his voice in the streets;
> he will nor break a bruised reed
>> or quench a smouldering wick,
> till he brings justice to victory;
>> and in his name will the Gentiles hope.'
>
> (Mat. 12.18–21, quoting Isa. 42.1–4)

Jesus was ordained as a Servant who, according to Isaiah, would know opposition and suffering, who would not be a triumphant Messiah, but a 'man of sorrows and acquainted with grief' (Isa. 52.13–53.12)

Christ's ordination at baptism consecrated him to a struggle which extended to death on the cross. Through this messianic consecration in baptism and the prophecy of Isaiah which is fulfilled, Jesus, the suffering Servant of Yahweh, gave to all his ministry and that of the Church, its characteristic spirit of humility and gentleness.[7]

Christ and the ministry of the Church after him, is the servant chosen by the Father, his beloved with whom his soul is well pleased. Ministry comes from above; it is not delegated by the Christian community but is given by God to his Church and to the world. A vocation from the Father, ministry is a gift of the Holy Spirit. God consecrates those whom he chooses and calls; he spreads out his Spirit upon them so that they may proclaim the true faith to all men. A servant's ministry does not delight in wrangles or cries, and is not heard in the streets; it is a humble, faithful ambassadorship for the Father, who likes to show his power in the weakness of his servants. Christ, and the ministry of the Church after him, respects man whom he must serve; there are no violent demands to obey a law; he watches for even the slightest sign of human good will. He does not break a bruised reed, he does not quench a smouldering wick. Gently he rekindles spiritual life in the hearts of those who are indifferent and lukewarm. He knows that through this careful patience, indulgence and the docility of charity, true faith may triumph, a triumph of love, humility and gentleness.

At his baptism Christ was ordained to his Messiah's ministry, as the suffering Servant of Yahweh, foretold by Isaiah. At his transfiguration he received confirmation of this ordination, as victorious and glorious Lord. Having been marked with the sign of the suffering Servant he was designated the Messiah king (Matt. 17.1–8).

Before his passion Christ received through his transfiguration assurance of the victory of the resurrection. As at his baptism it was in the presence of the messianic community, represented here by the three chief apostles, that he received the sign of his mission; the old covenant was also present in the appearance of Moses and Elijah. The ministry of Christ the Lord sums up all the law and the prophets and begins the ministry of the new covenant, the apostolic ministry of the Church. At that sight Peter wanted to place the holy ones in booths, recalling the desert tabernacle, the dwelling place of God and a sacred sign in the midst of the people. But it was interrupted by the appearance of the bright cloud which overshadowed them. The bright cloud, which accompanied God's people in the desert, was the sign of God's presence. The phenomenon can be related to the appearance of the dove at the baptism of Jesus, symbolizing the descent of the

Holy Spirit consecrating the Son to his mission as Servant. The Holy Spirit, in the form of the bright cloud of the old covenant enveloped Christ, Moses, Elijah, Peter, James and John, uniting the two convenants in Christ, the one prophet, priest and king of the renewed people of God. The Father's voice was heard, repeating the words of the baptism, again designating Christ the Messiah: 'This is my beloved Son, with whom I am well pleased; listen to him' (Mat. 17.5).

The disciples were fearful at that voice and fell to the ground in awe, but Christ raised them up and reassured them. The vision was over; they had to go back down the mountain and keep the secret until the resurrection. For the time being they had to commit themselves with Christ to the way of the passion. It was not possible for them to do what Peter wanted and remain in contemplation of Christ by building a tabernacle, as in the desert. They had to listen to the Messiah, obey him and follow him along the painful way of the cross. To attain his celestial, glorious ministry, Christ had to give himself voluntarily to death. Through that he showed the way to all ministry in the Church, which has to pass through renunciation and sacrifice to arrive at victory in God's terms. Ministry in the Church is not simply resting in God in contemplation, it is also a battle for Christ's redemption to reach all men, through the renunciation, sacrifice and suffering of his ministers. If there are moments of transfiguration for the ministry, for example in the liturgy, they are always fleeting anticipation of the peace and joy of God's kingdom; it is impossible to stay still, as St. Peter wished, without betraying the condition of ministry; it is necessary to come back down, strong in the vision of God, to bring his word to men.

If the transfiguration brought Christ and the apostles the promise of the resurrection, it was to strengthen them for the battle of the passion, the climax of Christ's ministry.

Baptism itself had already set Christ on the path of battle. The transfiguration was to be followed by the passion, baptism was followed by temptation in the wilderness. These two parallel moments in the designation of Christ as the suffering Servant and as the Messiah king were to lead him to his militant ministry which was the Son's sacrifice for, and service to, man. As soon as he was invested with his ministry as Servant, by the word of the Father and the power of the

Spirit, 'Jesus was led up by the Spirit into the wilderness to be tempted by the devil' (Mat. 4.1–11). After the transfiguration Christ was to assume man's condition to the end in passing through death; after his baptism he was to reveal his full humanity immediately in undergoing the trials of temptation, with which all men are familiar.[8]

Christ underwent the three temptations of nature, pride and power. All men are susceptible to these three temptations, but most particularly the ministers of the Church. Like Christ they must be exemplary witnesses who show in their lives that God is their strength and fully satisfies them. They have no cause to worry about the needs of their human nature; God feeds them and takes care of them. They must beware of pride which may be fostered by their privileged position: ministry gives them no rights at all. Finally they must renounce all human authority to make it quite clear that their only strength comes from God alone: their only power is spiritual, the power of God's word which it is their mission to proclaim in the world.

In his action of washing the disciples' feet Christ gave deep significance to his ministry in the Church and invited all ministers to follow his example to become true signs and instruments of this unique ministry (John 13.1–10).

Before he left this world to go to the Father, Christ gave his apostles a sign of perfect love which summed up his whole ministry. 'Having loved his own who were in the world, Jesus loved them to the end' (John 13.1). He knew that the Father had placed everything in his hands. Here St. John's Gospel expresses the fullness of Christ's ministry. As a plenipotentiary minister the Son of God received from his Father all power to proclaim peace to the world and to bring men to reconcilation with their Lord. Christ was conscious of this total power which made him 'the apostle and high priest of our confession' (Heb. 3.1). He knew that the Father had sent him to tell men the good news which they in turn would have to proclaim: he was the apostle of the faith we profess; he knew he was the supreme priest who would offer the perfect sacrifice and be the perpetual intercessor and our true advocate with the Father: he was the high priest of the faith we profess. He came from God as apostle and ambassador of the good news of salvation, and he returned to God as high priest and advocate of our communion with the Father. In the knowledge of the fullness of his ministry he was to show the apostles how they could become signs and instruments of that unique apostolate and priesthood which the Father had entrusted to them: he was going to wash their feet.[9]

Here he stooped to the level of a humble, faithful servant. Peter, knowing the greatness of his Master, did not want to permit such an action; but Jesus told him that he would understand afterwards. He would understand when he saw Christ reach the depths of humiliation in the sacrifice of the cross; he would understand when he himself, an apostle, would have to preside over the Church as a humble servant and accept the sacrifice of martyrdom.

Jesus replied to Peter's second refusal: 'If I do not wash you, you have no part in me' (John 13.8). Peter had to accept this token of charity and humility. As an apostle he could only be a sign and instrument of Christ's ministry in the Church if he accepted full participation in the service and sacrifice of his master. As a minister of the Church Peter had to be in complete communion with Christ who washed his disciples' feet in a token of charity, humility, service and sacrifice.

After the institution of the Eucharist, a dispute arose among the apostles as to which of them was to be regarded as the greatest (Luke 22.24–27). And Jesus answered them: 'The kings of the Gentiles exercise lordship over them; and those in authority over them are called benefactors. But not so with you; rather let the greatest among you become as the youngest, and the leader as one who serves. For which is the greater, one who sits at table, or one who serves? Is it not the one who sits at table? But I am among you as one who serves (*diakonôn*)'. Here Jesus is calling himself the 'deacon' of the apostles (the one who serves); the ministers of the Church, following the example of the Master, if they are to take part in his ministry, must serve their brothers as 'deacons'. Jesus ended the sign of washing their feet by saying: 'If I then, your Lord and Teacher, have washed your feet, you also ought to wash one another's feet. For I have given you an example, that you also should do as I have done to you'. This act of washing their feet can be seen as a sort of ordination of the apostles to their ministry, a sign and instrument of the unique ministry of Christ. Jesus consecrated his own to the ministry of the Church in a symbolic act through which they became deacons, servants in charity, humility and sacrifice.

The apostles, and later the ministers of the Church, would share in Christ's ministry if they followed his example: 'a servant is not greater than his master, nor is he who is sent greater than he who sent him' (John 13.16). If the Lord and Master of the Church was willing to be a servant, the apostles and ministers of the Church must do the same, to perform Christ's ministry properly. So ministers are in every sense signs and instruments of Christ's ministry amd may have faith in their Master's words. 'He who receives any one whom I send receives me, and he who receives me receives him who sent me' (John 13.10). The apostle and the minister consecrated by Christ's humble charity, which is symbolized in the washing of feet, being obedient to that order of service and sacrifice, as true deacons of Jesus the servant, bring to their ministry the actual ministry of the Lord. To receive them is to receive Christ who sent them; to hear them is to hear God himself. Jesus said to the disciples sent out on mission: 'He who hears you hears me, and he who rejects you rejects me, and he who rejects me rejects him who sent me' (Luke 10.16).

2

THE THREE FUNCTIONS
OF THE SERVANT

Tradition has given Christ's priesthood and ministry, which is shared by all Christians and the ministry in the Church, the titles of 'prophet, priest and king'. These names sum up the different aspects of Christ's priesthood and ministry, linking them to the old covenant where these three functions revealed God at work in and through his people.[10] Thus Christ appears as the Servant fulfilling the old covenant: he is the perfect successor to the prophets, priests and kings of the chosen people; he performs definitively the work which they began in the service of the living God. After him there was to be no further prophet, priest or king in the sense of the old covenant, but a prophetic, priestly and royal people: the whole Church and its ministers, the signs and instruments of Christ, the one prophet, priest and king.

Christ is a prophet because he proclaims the word of God in the power of the Spirit. From the age of twelve, when he went to Jerusalem for the first time, for the Passover, he took his place among the teachers, listening to them, asking questions and instructing them, and all those who heard him were amazed at his understanding and his answers (Luke 2.47).

Immediately after his baptism, the messianic anointing, and his temptation in the wilderness, his first struggle in his humanity, Jesus went back to Galilee 'in the power of the Spirit' (Luke 4.14) and he began his prophetic preaching: 'He taught in their synagogues, being glorified by all' (Luke 4.15). His ministry in Galilee was to be that of a prophet in the power of the Spirit. Luke the evangelist likes to underline the role of the Holy Spirit which accompanied Jesus in his ministry. The prophet is a man of the Word and of the Spirit.

In the synagogue at Nazareth Jesus read from the book of Isaiah: 'The Spirit of the Lord is upon me, because he has anointed me to preach good news to the poor. He has sent me to proclaim release to the captives and recovering of sight to the blind, to set at liberty those who are oppressed, to proclaim the acceptable year of the Lord' (Luke 4.18–19, quoting Isa. 61.1–2).

He described himself as a prophet full of the Spirit, anointed in baptism, who preached the gospel and grace to all men: 'Today this scripture has been fulfilled in your hearing' (Luke 4.21). They all spoke well of him and wondered at the words of grace which he spoke. They were amazed that the man they knew well could speak in such a way; and already doubt was creeping into their hearts: 'Is not this Joseph's son?' Is he not like us, this prophet who tries to show himself superior to us? And Jesus expounded to them the tragic situation of the prophet who is never well received by those closest to him: 'Truly, I say to you, no prophet is acceptable in his own country' (Luke 4.14). He revealed the mysterious ways of God in making his word effective outside the land of his prophets. Elijah was sent to a widow in Zarephath, in the land of Sidon, at a time when there were many widows in Israel. It is a mysterious part of the prophet's vocation to see his word bear fruit where he has sown nothing. The prophet has to serve the universality of God's salvation. He is led where he did not intend to go. He must recognize the traces of God's movements beyond the limits of his people.[11]

But this universalism of the prophet's ministry and preaching is not readily accepted by the intransigents. It constitutes a judgement on their hardness of heart. And that is why Christ's early preaching aroused fury in the synagogue at Nazareth. Admiration gave way to anger. They were proud of their local son, but were unable to accept the judgement of God's word. So they pushed Jesus to a precipice to throw him over. The Servant's prophetic ministry led him to suffering and death; but God was watching over him and protecting him: 'Passing through the midst of them he went away' (Luke 4.30).

Throughout his ministry in Galilee Jesus was to experience these tragic consequences of his preaching at the same time as the joy brought by the fruits of conversion and healing. His prophetic ministry did not allow any compromise with the world, which was why the Pharisees finally tried to get him out of Galilee on the pretext that Herod wanted to kill him (Luke 13.31). But he had to continue his ministry despite the threats; he had to follow the road which would take him to Jerusalem 'for it cannot be that a prophet should perish away from Jerusalem' (Luke 13.33).

After Christ the prophetic ministry of the Church provoked opposition, persecution and at times martyrdom, because it had that universalist character which at times judges the orthodox and upsets them, and because it allowed no compromise with the Pharisees or politicians. The prophetic ministry is completely free and universal, having the freedom and universality of God's word.

If the prophet is a man of God's word he is also a man of the Spirit. It was in the power of the Spirit that Christ the prophet proclaimed the free and universal word of God. Christ as prophet was a witness to the authenticity of the life of the Spirit. Religious institutions, legalistic observances, moralistic demands, ritualistic practices are in no way assurances of authentic communion with the living God. Only the life of the Spirit which bears the fruits of love allows a true relation of faith with God. Christ did not condemn institutions, laws, morality or liturgy as such; they are useful provided they are full of the Holy Spirit. The Holy Spirit must give life to religion for it to become a living relationship with God. Renewal in the Holy Spirit is essential for the institution to remain a living means of coming to God, an effective sign of his presence.

The prophet of the old covenant was not opposed to priestly and liturgical institutions; he denounced the rigidity, hypocrisy and lack of authenticity, which were due to man's infidelity in relying on his own works rather than on the grace of God. The prophet of the old covenant was raised up by God to give life to the religious institution when it was falling into formalism and legalism. The prophets proclaimed the supremacy of love over sacrifice; they did not want to suppress liturgical sacrifice but to enliven it by the Spirit of love which alone could make it authentic and effective.

Thus in the same way Christ the prophet did not come to establish the law but to fulfil it. He revealed its whole inner nature and showed its unity in loving God and one's neighbour. The whole sermon on the mount (Mat. 5.7) is a reiteration of the law of the old covenant in a spiritual sense; Christ gave new life to the law through the spirit of charity.

Talking about the commandment 'Thou shalt not kill', for example, Jesus showed that anger comes from the same source as murder, and from the same desire to suppress someone else. In the same way he gave Christians the command to be reconciled. It is not just a question of forgiving but also of being forgiven. So he said: 'If you are offering your gift at the altar, and there remember that your brother has something against you, leave your gift there before the altar and go; first be reconciled to your brother, and then come and offer your gift' (Mat. 5.23–24). The ritual act of the offering must be internalized through mercy; liturgical sacrifice only has a sense of communion with God if the believer is committed to that reconciliation which restores his communion with his neighbour. The Holy Spirit must come and bring to life the religious intention of anyone who wants to make a liturgical offering. Rather than make this liturgical sacrifice in a state of tension with one's neighbour, it is better to leave the offering at the altar provisionally and go and be reconciled first. Not just forgive, but seek forgiveness if someone else has cause for complaint against you. Then, in this new situation of fellowship which has been restored through mercy on both sides, we may come back to the altar for the liturgical act which is now full of true charity, the fruit of the Spirit.[12]

Christ was not making an opposition here between liturgy and love; he did not say that it was better not to make offerings in order to exercise charity; he united liturgy and charity; he showed that the liturgical sacrifice must be internalized by an act of reconciliation with one's neighbour, and that communion with God through the liturgy is only possible if it presupposes communion with one another in love. When reconciliation is complete, liturgical sacrifices takes on its full meaning in the Holy Spirit bringing its fruits of love. Here Christ showed the true relation between the demands of the prophet, thirsty for authenticity in the Spirit and for truth according to God's word, and the demands of the liturgy, which can only be performed in this obedience to the Spirit and to the word.[13]

In his conversation with the woman of Samaria Jesus spoke of worshipping in spirit and in truth (John 4.23). This was not to condemn the liturgical institutions of the Jews. The Samaritans worshipped the Father on Mount Gerizim and the Jews worshipped him at Jerusalem. The Samaritans worshipped God without knowledge of true faith; the Jews, on the other hand, worshipped the God they knew (John 4.22). Jesus placed himself firmly within the Jewish religious institution, as opposed to the Samaritans, who were considered heretics, although they were true worshippers of God. But he extended the worship of the living God to the whole universe and above all he described this worship as being renewed from within by the Spirit and truth. Once again it is on the basis of the orthodox Jewish religious institution that Christ delivered his prophetic message, which was to internalize and universalize it: 'The hour is coming when neither on this mountain (Gerizim) nor in Jerusalem will you worship the Father.... the hour is coming, and now is, when the true worshippers will worship the Father in spirit and truth, for such the Father seeks to worship him. God is spirit, and those who worship him must worship him in spirit and in truth' (John 4.21–24). True worship, instituted by Christ, is no longer confined to fixed places, it is universal, for the Spirit blows where it wills and truth will be proclaimed throughout all the earth. It is also worship imbued with the power of the Holy Spirit and the truth of Christ: it is the Spirit who inspires and brings to life Christian prayer and it is truth revealed in Christ which gives it its language and meaning.

Thus, in the Church, prophetic ministry, the sign and the instrument of the ministry of Christ the prophet, does not stand in opposition to liturgical ministry; it brings it to life through the Spirit and truth, through the Holy Spirit and the word of God. The oppositions spirit-liturgy, freedom-tradition and prophet-priest must be abolished. Rather they are complementary terms, the first giving life to the second which gives it its support and expression. The institution needs the prophet to give it life and to keep on internalizing it; the prophet needs the institution to pass on his message in the continuing life of the people of God.

Christ the prophet is God's spokesman transmitting his word in the power of the Holy Spirit to renew the life of God's people. Prophetic ministry in the Church is to serve the word proclaimed with the force of the Holy Spirit, which actually revives, enlivens and internalizes anew ecclesiastical and liturgical institutions, a sign of the Lord's faithfulness and his continuing presence in his Body, the Church.

The manifestation of Christ as Messiah king at the transfiguration occurs in the Gospels between the two occasions when the passion and the resurrection are foretold: 'From that time Jesus began to show his disciples that he must go to Jerusalem and suffer many things from the elders and chief priests and scribes, and be killed, and on the third day be raised' (Mat. 16.21). This first foretelling of the passion and resurrection is followed by the invitation to the disciples to follow Christ in his sacrifice: 'If any man could come after me, let him deny himself and take up his cross and follow me. For whoever would save his life will lose it, and whoever loses his life for my sake will find it' (Mat. 16.24–25).

At his baptism Jesus received messianic anointing; this was at once made manifest in his prophetic ministry, when in the power of the Holy Spirit he proclaimed God's word for the renewal of Israel. This prophetic ministry, a testimony to the universality and the freedom of God's word, set Christ on the way to persecution and suffering; his first preaching at Nazareth was an example of it. But it is after the transfiguration, which renewed the messianic anointing, that events began to speed up and Christ foretold very clearly his death and resurrection. At the same time he invited his disciples to share in his sacrifice, to take up their cross, deny themselves and lose their lives in order to regain them. From the moment of transfiguration, when the Father again designated Jesus the Servant: 'my beloved Son with whom I am well pleased', when God gave him the advance sign of the resurrection, Christ set out along the way to his passion and asked his disciples to share it, to be worthy of following him. He was going to leave Galilee for Jerusalem where it befitted prophets to perish.

The transfiguration marked a new stage in Christ's ministry. After his baptismal anointing he worked as a prophet, proclaiming the word, along with miraculous signs in the power of the Spirit; after the illumination of the transfiguration, he was also to act as a priest, renouncing himself, giving himself as a sacrifice, carrying his cross and losing his life to regain it in the resurrection. The two stages are not absolutely distinct. Christ's prophetic ministry already implied his suffering. But at the time of the transfiguration the drama of the passion was precipitated. Henceforth Christ appeared in his priestly ministry which completed his prophetic ministry. Christ was a priest because he gave himself for others, went to the sacrifice of the cross and lost his life in order regain it. Just as they had been called to share his prophetic ministry in proclaiming Christ's word, so the apostles were called to share his priestly ministry, taking up their cross to follow him in his passion, renouncing themselves, sacrificing themselves for others and losing their lives in order to regain them.

Christ was a priest because in his passion he offered the perfect sacrifice of his life for the salvation of mankind, and in his heavenly intercession he prays that all men may receive this salvation and Christians may be sanctified. The priestly prayer which he offered before his passion (John 17) fully sums up his priestly ministry 'Sanctify them in the truth; thy word is truth. As thou didst send me into the world, so I have sent them into the world. And for their sake I consecrate myself, that they also may be consecrated in truth' (John 17.17–19). Here Christ is interceding with the Father as a priest. He asks that the apostles be sanctified in the word of truth, so that they may accomplish their mission in the world in his name. They were to continue the ministry of the Son sent by the Father. And so that they might thus be sanctified by the word of truth, Christ himself was sanctified: he offered himself in the sacrifice of his life, which constituted his supreme intercession for his people.

Christ's priesthood is not the same as the priesthood of the old covenant, but it is the fulfilment of it. The priests of the old covenant offered symbolic sacrifices which signified man's desire to repent, to come back to God and to give himself to live in communion with him. But these liturgical sacrifices remained external to priest and believer; offerings could not bring about the spiritual commitment of the heart. Periodically prophets would denounce the formalism of sacrifices which did not impose any commitment on the conscience. The psalmist cried:

> 'Thou hast no delight in sacrifice;
>> were I to give a burnt offering,
>> thou wouldst not be pleased.
> The sacrifice acceptable to God is a broken spirit;
>> a broken and contrite heart, O God, thou wilt not
>> despise.' (Ps. 51.16–17)

Even the most complete liturgical sacrifice, a burnt offering, was not pleasing to God if it did not bring with it the consecration of the heart and spirit. But at the same time as criticizing priesthood and sacrifice for being powerless to bring conscience into the offering to God, the psalmist prophesied the great rebuilding of Jerusalem, where the complete and perfect oblation would become possible:

> 'Do good to Zion in thy good pleasure;
>   rebuild the walls of Jerusalem,
> then wilt thou delight in right sacrifices,
>   in burnt offerings and whole burnt offerings...'
> (Ps. 51.18–10)

With the coming of the Messiah Jerusalem would be rebuilt; sacrifices would be acceptable because they would indeed lead the hearts and spirits of believers to be offered in complete oblation. Christ fulfilled this prophesy. His sacrifice was not external, like that of the priests of the old covenant. His sacrifice was the offering of himself, his life and his death to the Father as a living intercession for all men. Priesthood and sacrifice are a single entity in Christ, perfectly internalized and spiritual.[14]

According to the Epistle to the Hebrews, Christ the priest came to abolish the old order, that of the law, in order to establish the new order, that of the Gospel:

> 'Sacrifices and offerings thou hast desired,
> but a body hast thou prepared for me;
> in burnt offerings and sin offerings thou hast taken
>   no pleasure.
> Then I said, "Lo, I have come to do thy will, O God"
> (Heb. 10.5–7; Ps. 40.6–8).

The sacrifice of the new covenant desired by and pleasing to God was the voluntary offering of his body by Christ the priest: 'A body hast thou prepared for me... I said "Lo I have come to do thy will, O God..."'. Christ replaced the external liturgical sacrifices of the old covenant by the offering of his own body. The sacrifice of the new covenant is the identicalness of priest and offering, the total gift of Christ who offers his whole being to the Father and who is totally disposed to do his will. Christ's sacrifice is perfect and definitive because it is the obedience of the Son, in offering his whole being to carry out his Father's will.[15] Our sanctification will consist essentially in uniting ourselves with Christ in his obedience and his offering. There are no possible external sacrifices for us; there is only the gift of ourselves in obedience, in union with Christ who offered himself once for all in perfect obedience. Sacrifice is essentially an offering of man's whole being, in union with Christ's unique and perfect sacrifice, to fulfil the Father's will in obedience unto death; and this sacrifice of the whole being united with Christ becomes the valid content of all liturgical sacrifice. This is why the word sacrifice in the New Testament is applied not to a liturgical act of the Christian community, but to the offering of the Christian's being, his life and obedience. That is the sacrifice that is necessarily contained in all liturgy.

'I appeal to you, brethren', writes St. Paul, 'by the mercies of God, to present your bodies as a living sacrifice, holy and acceptable to God, which is your spiritual worship' (Rom. 12.1). This verse expresses clearly the nature and meaning of the priesthood of the new covenant, whether it be the royal priesthood of all Christians, or the ministry in its priestly aspect as the sign and instrument of the unique priesthood of Christ. Just as Christ the priest offered himself for his Father's glory and man's salvation, so Christians, whether lay or ordained, according to their own vocation, must see their priesthood as a sacrifice of their whole person. The sacrifice of the Christian priesthood is not an external sacrifice requiring personal commitment but the internal offering of the whole person himself.[16] There is no sacrifice other than the living, holy sacrifice of Christians, in union with the unique sacrifice of Christ. This sacrifice is living in that it is the offering of one's whole life; the sacrifice is holy in that it is the offering of sanctification. This sacrifice alone is pleasing to God, since, like Christ's, it is not an external sacrifice which does not affect the individual, but an internal sacrifice which involves the commitment of a sanctified life.

This new conception of Christian sacrifice is the starting point for understanding the royal priesthood of all believers and ministry in the Church. Christian liturgy and its sacrificial nature should be understood on the basis of this new Christian idea of sacrifice: before liturgical sacrifice, there must be a total sacrifice of the Christian life, and it necessarily contains this.

The priesthood of Christ is described in the Epistle to the Hebrews with reference to the rite of the Atonement, celebrated each year by the Jewish high priest. Christ offered the perfect and definitive sacrifice of his whole being in obedience to the Father, the one living, holy and acceptable sacrifice. Then, with the sign of that sacrifice which marked humanity for ever, he entered the Holy of Holies, God's presence, on the day of his ascension. As the high priest of Israel would enter the Holy of Holies once a year, with the blood of an external sacrifice for the sins of the people, so Christ the high priest of rewards to come, entered the heavenly Holy of Holies, on the day of his ascension, once for all, with his own blood, the memorial of the sacrifice of his body for mankind's eternal redemption.[17] Thus Christ's body, the sign of his perfect sacrifice, purifies our conscience from dead works, so that we may worship the living God. Thanks to his sacrifice, the offering of himself in intercession for us, Christ our high priest leads us in his footsteps, so that we in turn may commit our conscience through a total sacrifice in which we will be purified and able to offer the spiritual worship to the living God, in spirit and in truth, to which we are called.

Thus Christ's perfect and definitive priesthood is fulfilled in two stages: in the sacrifice of the cross, a total offering of himself, and in heavenly intercession, a perpetual memorial of his sacrifice for man's salvation and sanctification. Christian priesthood is, in the communion of Christ, commitment to a total sacrifice of one's life and to fervent intercession for mankind. This priesthood is performed in everyday existence and in a life of prayer. In his very existence, as in prayer, the Christian offers his body as a living holy sacrifice. Ministers are signs and instruments of Christ's unique and perfect priesthood in the service of their brethren, which extends to the free sacrifice of their whole life, and in prayers of intercession, which bring before God all who are entrusted to them, for their salvation and sanctification.

Christ's place in the Church is the place of the king of the old covenant. As God's anointed, the king belonged to the Lord and was full of the Spirit. He represented the people before God and was the channel for the Lord's blessing on his people. He had a function in worship and could bless the assembly of Israel (1 Kings 8.14). The king represented God in his authority and was the forerunner of the Messiah; thus in Psalm 45 the king is called 'divine':

'Your divine throne endures for ever and ever.
Your royal sceptre is a sceptre of equity;

You love righteousness and hate wickedness.
Therefore God, your God, has anointed you
with the oil of gladness above your fellows;
your robes are all fragrant with myrrh and aloes and
  cassia.' (Ps. 45.6–8).

Through his resurrection and ascension Christ, the Messiah and Servant, became king of the Church and of the universe. He sits as eternal king at the Father's right hand. There he represents the whole Church for whom he intercedes, recalling his unique sacrifice. He leads his people and fills them with the blessings of the Holy Spirit. It was as king that at Pentecost Christ sent the Holy Spirit upon his apostles to give them a universal mission among men, to make them and their successors his ambassadors in the church and in the world.

During his earthly life the incarnate Son of God presented himself as the shepherd-king of his people: 'I am the good shepherd' (John 10.1–18). In assuming this title Christ reveals his identity as Messiah-king.[18] He is the good shepherd because he gives his life for his sheep. The hired shepherd tries to escape in times of difficulty, abandoning the sheep which are not his. But the good shepherd cares for his sheep and sacrifices himself to save them. His life is not taken from him, he gives it of his own accord. If he does leave the flock for a while it is to go and look for the lost sheep, putting his own life in danger. He knows his sheep and is known by them. His authority is fully recognized because it stems from a generous, self-sacrificing love. The sheep do not heed a stranger, but they do listen to the voice of the good shepherd and follow him out of the fold, wherever he wants to lead them. They follow him confidently because they know his voice. The good shepherd is not just concerned with the sheep of that fold; he has other sheep to lead; they will heed his voice and there will be one flock and one shepherd. Here Christ refers to the universal nature of the Church; his ministry is not solely concerned with the fold of the flock of Israel; Christ has his followers in the whole world and he must lead them all to the kingdom. He is not to lead all the sheep into the fold of Israel, but he must bring the flock out of its fold and lead it throughout the world, drawing in the other sheep, who are not of this fold, in the progress of the whole of the universal flock towards the kingdom of God.

Christ's royal authority is his because he has given his life for all men, as the good shepherd for his sheep; he knows his own and they know him, in a communion of life and love; men recognize his voice and his words as those of a genuine shepherd; he does not compel anyone to enter the narrow confines of a human institution, but he leads all who belong to him in the movement of the universal Church.

Christ's royal ministry is founded entirely on his sacrifice, on his knowing his own in love, on the word by which he leads them to the kingdom. Ministry in the Church is essentially a pastoral function, the mission and actions of a shepherd. The pastor is the minister, the sign and instrument of the unique shepherd. He can lead with authority those who are entrusted to him only if he sacrifices himself for them, if he gives his life for those he loves; he can only be the minister of Christ the shepherd if he knows the faithful with love, if he knows each one by name in a communion of life, joy and suffering; he can only be the minister of Christ the king if his authority is based on the word of God, for the sheep of the flock know only the voice of Christ the good shepherd, whom alone they can truly obey; he can only be the minister of the Lord of the whole Church if he leads his flock out of the fold to take them into the world where other sheep will join him, thanks to the universal mission of Christ, the good shepherd of all mankind.

Royal ministry in the Church, the sign and instrument of the unique ministry of Christ the King, is thus based on sacrifice, communion, word and mission; it is only on these foundations that authoritative ministry is possible; the pastor is a man who gives himself for all, who has compassion on each one, who leads Christian people by God's word, taking them to minister to the world.

This function of shepherd-king is fulfilled in the sacrifice of the cross where Christ gave his life to the end. The shepherd sacrificed himself for the sheep of his flock and became the slaughtered lamb. St. John gives a profound theological significance to the different aspects of the crucifixion. For him Christ fulfilled on the cross the prophecy of the passover lamb, whose blood had marked the doors of the Israelites in Egypt, to deliver them. Christ is the new and definitive passover lamb by whose blood men will be delivered. According to John he was crucified on the day of the preparation for the Passover, the day when the passover meal was prepared, to take place after sunset. Jesus was to be slaughtered on the cross at the time when the paschal lamb was slaughtered for the liturgical meal of the Passover. Christ is the true and definitive paschal lamb who takes away the sin of the world. Not a bone of him was broken (John 19.36) like the passover lamb (Exod. 12.46). Christ the shepherd-king became the slaughtered lamb, because he was the suffering servant foretold by Isaiah (53). Christ fulfilled his ministry of Messiah-king and as the good shepherd in giving himself as a sacrifice, like the paschal lamb taking away the sin of the world. His ministry was essentially sacrifice and service. It was at the sixth hour when the Jews were preparing to kill the passover lamb that Pilate prophesied saying to the Jews: 'Behold your king'. And they replied:'Away with him, away with him, crucify him!' (John 19.14–15). The shepherd-king had to die like the slaughtered lamb. His kingship, his royal ministry and his authority were founded on his sacrifice.[19]

Pilate had written on the cross: 'Jesus of Nazareth, the King of the Jews' (John 19.19). In doing that he became the unknowing instrument of God's word. The man he had already presented as 'the man', then as 'king' (John 19.5–14) was given this title on the cross in his humanity and in his kingship. The soldiers had also humiliated him by dressing him in purple and calling him king. Even those who thought they were humiliating Christ were unwittingly moved to proclaim his kingship. And they all proclaimed this royal function of Christ in the setting that befitted him and was foreseen, according to God's will. Indeed Christ's royal ministry can only be based on the humiliation, suffering and sacrifice of the passion and the cross. He is only the Messiah-king because he is the suffering servant; he is only the good shepherd because he is slaughtered like the passover lamb.

In another part of the crucifixion narrative (John 19.23–24) Jesus appears in his priestly ministry. The reference to the tunic without seam, for which the soldiers cast lots, is reminiscent of the robe of the Jewish high priest, which had to be without seam.[20] In this precise detail of clothing the evangelist tends to show Christ as the true and definitive high priest of the people, who makes the perfect, perpetual expiation. Christ on the cross is the eternal high priest who offers himself as the passover lamb. Priesthood and sacrifice are a single entity.

Thus Christ fulfils the prophecies: he is simultaneously lamb, king and high priest; in his sacrifice on the cross he unites his prophetic, priestly and royal ministries. He fulfils the word of God, as a perfect prophet, by the definitive sacrifice which he slaughters, as both eternal priest and redeeming victim; he establishes his royal authority of the good shepherd by giving his life as the paschal lamb. Christ on the cross is the faithful prophet, sacrificed priest and obedient king. The only true ministry in the Church is as a sign and instrument of that prophet and priest and the king who was crucified and brought to life again.[21]

PART TWO

THE APOSTOLIC MINISTRY

3

THE APOSTLES:
AMBASSADORS AND STEWARDS

Since the incarnation and the unique sacrifice of the cross
there has been only one possible priest, one acceptable offering: Christ himself, the high priest of rewards to come and
heavenly intercessor, the lamb slaughtered as a living
memorial before the Father. It is through Christ that we
receive the Holy Spirit and all the blessings given to us by the
Father. It is through Christ that with the strength of the Holy
Spirit we can offer ourselves to God in prayer and praise.
Christ is the one mediator between God and man. Ministry in
the Church is the sign and instrument of this unique
mediation.

Christ founded the ministry in the Church by instituting
the college of the twelve apostles, to whom he entrusted the
mission of being ambassadors in his name.[1] In the institution
of the college of the twelve there are some elements which can
be handed on and some which cannot. The twelve represent
the new Israel, they symbolize the twelve tribes of the people
of God, they are the foundations of the Church because they
were eyewitnesses to the life, passion and resurrection of
Christ. This aspect of the apostolic ministry cannot be
handed on. But the apostles were sent out into the world to
preach the Gospel, to baptize and celebrate the Eucharist, to
give the Holy Spirit in the laying on of hands, to forgive men
their sins and to bring together and build up the Church.
These elements of their ministry were transmitted to others,
to their closest fellow-workers and to the bishops, priests and
deacons whom they appointed to the local Churches.

The mission of the Twelve is unique in that they were the

foundation and first authorities of the Church, but it was to be extended to others insofar as they were Christ's ambassadors sent to proclaim in his name: 'The kingdom of God has come near to you' (Luke 10.9). The apostles and the ministers who succeeded them were sent by Christ: 'As the Father has sent me, even so I send you', they were told by the risen Christ (John 20.21). The Father sent his Son to preach the Gospel in the power of the Spirit, to live, die and rise again for the salvation of all mankind. Following this mission given to the Son by the Father, in the power of the Spirit, the Son in turn sent the apostles and their successors to preach salvation in the world. The apostles and their successors were ambassadors of Christ: they could speak and act in his name and were the signs and instruments of his presence, his word and his work in the world.

Before his ascension, by the power which he has in earth and heaven, Christ gave them full powers to represent him in human form until the end of the world; he assured them of his presence and commanded them to preach and baptize and to make disciples in all nations: 'All authority in heaven and on earth has been given to me. Go therefore and make disciples of all nations, baptizing them in the name of the Father and of the Son and of the Holy Spirit, teaching them to observe all that I have commanded you; and lo, I am with you always, to the close of the age' (Matt. 28.18–20). In their prophetic ministry of preaching the Gospel, apostles and ministers are promised that Christ is present by his word in their words: 'He who hears you hears me', he said to the Seventy, 'and he who rejects you rejects me, and he who rejects me rejects him who sent me' (Luke 10.16; see Matt. 10.40–42, Mark 9.35–37, Luke 9. 46–48, John 13.20). To receive a minister as an ambassador of Christ and hear him preaching his word, is to receive and hear Christ himself; to reject him is to reject Christ and the Father who sent him. 'He who receives a prophet (a minister of God's word) because he is a prophet shall receive a prophet's reward, and he who receives a righteous man (a disciple of Christ) because he is a righteous man shall receive a righteous man's reward' (Matt. 10.41). Apostles, prophets and ministers must be received in their own ministry, which is that of being ambassadors of Christ, in the same way as Christians must be received as Christ's disciples.

This presence of Christ in apostles or ministers, in that they are prophets of God's word, is thus very strongly affirmed in the Gospels; it gives them an authority which reveals that of Christ, whose signs and instruments they are. But it must straightway be remembered that this authority of Christ's prescence and his word is only accorded to apostles and ministers on condition they are humble. It is striking to note that Christ, underlining the authority of the twelve, reminds them at the same time that they must be 'little ones'. He compares them to children (Matt. 10.40–42; Mark 9.33–37; Luke 9.46–48); they were arguing as to who was the greatest and he told them: 'He who is least among you all is the one who is great' (Luke 9.48). The apostle or minister, who represents Christ and speaks in his name only has his authority if he makes himself the last and the servant of all: 'If anyone would be first', Christ said to them, 'he must be the last of all and the servant of all' (Mark 9.35). Here again we see that the minister can only be an authentic sign and instrument of Christ, and take on the authority of his word and presence, if he is humble and small, a servant. Humility and authority necessarily go together for a minister of the Church. When he washed their feet Christ showed his apostles that their ministerial authority was that of humble servants who give themselves and sacrifice themselves for others.

Christ summed up this duty of the minister to represent the work of God himself in the world, in his promise to Peter, then to all the apostles and ministers: 'I will give you the keys of the kingdom of heaven, and whatever you bind on earth shall be bound in heaven, and whatever you loose on earth shall be loosed in heaven' (Matt. 16.19 and 18.18). Peter, as the first of the apostles, but having everything in common with them all, received the keys from the steward of God's house. His ministry gave him the duty and service to handle the goods of that house in the name of his master.[2]

That responsibility for showing mercy and for reconciliation lies in having to loose men from the chains of sin, through the liberating power of the Gospel. It applies to the whole of the Church's ministry: doctrinal, sacramental and pastoral; it sums up the services of the word, the sacraments, and of unity. Every minister shares this power, not equally, but according to the office entrusted to him, the extent of the responsibility invested in him, and the importance of the flock which he is sent to guard as a shepherd. In the two passages we have referred to (Matt. 16.19 and 18.18), we see that Christ promised the ministry of stewardship of God's house first to Peter, as head of the college of apostles, then to the apostles and to all the ministers. There is a single power of the Gospel which remits sins, but a diversity of ministers, duties and responsibilities. This is not the place to talk of Peter's function in the apostolic college and of the possibility of succession to his office.[3] We shall come back to that later. It is enough to note here that the unique evangelistic power to remit sins varies according to offices in the Church and that this power contains in itself the whole apostolic ministry of the Church: word, sacraments, unity. It would be wrong to interpret this promise in the restricted sense of absolution. Elsewhere Christ bestows the power of forgiving sins in the true sense of the word (John 20.23), but here it is a question of the whole of the Gospel ministry, which consists of freeing men according to the different means of grace provided by God. In all these aspects of the unique apostolic ministry of the Gospel in the Church, ministers speak and act as signs and instruments of Christ, the one prophet, priest and king of the Church.

In the apostles the whole existence of the Church has its origin. But here we have to see how ministry developed in the Church beginning with the twelve. Indeed, if the twelve form the initial centre of the whole new Israel, as God's people, the Church's ministry also originates with them. The ministry of the twelve was not only exercised at the beginning of the Church, but, in the same way as Christ continues to act in the Church as the one prophet, priest and king, the apostles also remain present in the Church to rule it, as a college subordinate to Christ, through their witness which re-echoes in New Testament writing and through their prayers in communion with Christ before the Father. If in its liturgy the Church makes memorial of the apostles in a very special way, it is because of its belief in their living presence in the Body of Christ to govern it by their witness and to help it through their intercession.

The apostles received from Christ the mission to found and extend the early Church by their word, which conveyed God's word, by the celebration of Christ's sacraments and by exercising the Spirit's authority in charity, with the aim of unity. They were essentially made to be misionaries, founders and pastors. Insofar as they transmitted God's word while inspired by the Holy Spirit, their mission remains unique, permanent and unable to be handed on; their mission is set down in the books of the New Testament; nothing could be added which has the force of the inspired word of God; this witness remains alive and permanent in the Church.[4] But the apostles themselves appointed their fellow workers and their successors. Part of their ministry could be handed on: their mission had to be pursued on the basis of their first, unique witness of the life, death and resurrection of Christ; other Churches had to be founded as well as those which they themselves founded along the Mediterranean coast; these Churches had to be led, presided over and ruled by pastors, who were continuing the apostles' ministry, with the authority of their living witness and as ambassadors of Christ, the one shepherd and bishop of the faithful (1 Pet. 2.25).

The college of the twelve, instituted by Christ as the foundation for the new Israel, to carry out the Gospel mission to found and rule over Churches, was joined by other apostles, chosen directly by Christ himself in glory, or elected by Christ's apostles. Matthias and Paul appear as chosen by Christ himself in glory.

The college was diminished by the betrayal of Judas and the completeness desired by Christ had to be recovered; it was out of this completeness that was to spring the mission ordered by Christ and the diversity of ministry in the Church. The apostolic ministry could not be reduced, even to eleven apostles; even if Peter had the function of leadership among the apostles, the ministry could not be centred on him, nor on any other apostle or group of apostles. It is in the totality of the apostolic college that the apostolic ministry is complete. That is why Peter himself as their leader, reminded the eleven and the brethren of the infant Church that Judas had to be replaced, so that the completeness of the apostolic ministry instituted by Christ could be symbolized by the college of the twelve. The choice of Matthias echoes the old practices of Judaism and of the Qumran community (Acts 1.15–26).[5] Peter recalled that Judas had received 'a share in this ministry', *kleros tes diakonias*; the ministry, diaconate and service was viewed as a whole, shared collegiately by the twelve, indicating the completeness of the ministry of the new Israel. Since this number symbolizes fullness they had to give Judas's share, his *kleros*, to another, And Peter quoted the Scripture: 'Let another his office take' (his *episkope*, or duty of overseeing). The order of this apostolic election, begun in Scripture, is continued by the indication of how the twelve should function: they are to bear witness to the resurrection of Christ, and sets out the conditions of this apostolate: to have been in the company of the apostles during the earthly life of Jesus, from his baptism by John until his ascension. Then comes the prayer: the apostles commit to God, who knows the hearts of all men, the choice between two candidates who fulfil the conditions of the apostolate of the twelve. The man elected will take 'the place in this ministry and apostleship from which Judas turned aside' (Acts 1.25). Here again we find underlined the fact of a collegiate apostolic ministry within which one place had been left vacant; it had to be filled so that the apostolate had its full complement. Finally, in the last act of this 'liturgy' (Scripture, designation of office, prayer)[6] they cast lots and Matthias is added to the number of the twelve apostles. This casting of lots to discover God's will was familiar from the Old Testament: it was consultation by the Urim and the Thummim. These objects which served to make known God's will by lot had been entrusted to the priests (Exod. 28.30, Lev.8.8, Deut. 33.8, Ezra 2.63; Neh. 7.65). It was a perfectly priestly function to consult the Lord in this way. So the apostles saw themselves as the authorized successors to the levitical priesthood in this function of seeking God's will by drawing lots after prayer. When Joshua was chosen to succeed Moses, the priest Eleazar had sought God's will according to the rite of the Urim. Yahweh had said to Moses: 'Take Joshua the son of Nun, a man in whom is the spirit, and lay your hand upon him; cause him to stand before Eleazar the priest and all the congregation, and you shall commission him in their sight. You shall invest him with some of your authority, that all the congregation of the people of Israel may obey. And he shall stand before Eleazar the priest, who shall inquire for him by the judgement of the Urim before the Lord...' (Num. 27.18–21). It was not a question of the choice of Joshua, which was already determined; Moses had to recognize the Spirit which was in him, lay his hand on him, give him his orders and invest him with some of his authority. The priest would seek God's will for him in the decisions he would have to take. We should note the difference between Joshua's admission to the ministry of Moses and that of Matthias to the twelve. Through the laying on of hands Joshua was dependent on the ministry of Moses, who handed over to him a part of his ministry and orders which he had to obey. Matthias did not receive the laying on of hands; he was not a successor to the apostles, dependent on their ministry. Like the twelve he was chosen directly by Christ by means of casting lots. He was Christ's apostle, of the same order as the others. The Lord made him enter the apostolic *diakonia* and *episkope*, of which he received his part in taking his place among the twelve. He was, as Paul was to call himself, 'an apostle — not from men nor through men, but through Jesus Christ and God the Father, who raised him from the dead' (Gal. 1.1).

Paul too was called an apostle of Christ, chosen directly; like Matthias, he had been the object of an extraordinary choice by Christ in glory. In the vision of Christ which converted him and in the words of Ananias this supernatural choice was revealed to him. Ananias laid hands on him for him to be healed and to receive the Holy Spirit; he baptized him. It was an act of healing and of initiation, not of apostolic succession. Moreover, Ananias was not an apostle (Acts 9.10–19). Paul was numbered among Christ's apostles through direct election, not through the intermediary of man (Gal. 1.1). He had been elected by Christ in glory to be 'a chosen instrument.. to carry [his] name before the Gentiles and kings and the sons of Israel' (Acts 9.15). Paul was to receive the laying on of hands with Barnabas at Antioch, before setting out on mission.

It may be asked why a thirteenth apostle of Christ was added to this college, since the completeness of the apostolate was to be found in the college of the twelve. That is a mystery, the reasons for which can be explored a little, without exhausting the subject. The instititution of the twelve, in the continuity of Israel, needed to be brought to life by the spiritual event which was the choice of Paul.[7] God, who desired the institution of the Church and traditional continuity in order to show his faithfulness, also desired the spiritual event and prophetic novelty to indicate his freedom.

God keeps his promises but he remains free in his sovereignty. The college of the twelve represents the apostolic institution from which the instititution of the Church originates; Paul's apostleship represents the spiritual event which underlies prophethood in the Church. It is a warning to the Church which, faithful to its apostolic institution, must always remain free to accept prophetic events in its midst. Secondly, the institution of the twelve could run the risk of turning in on itself, despite Christ's commands. The twelve could remain too exclusively in the service of the Old Israel, too attached to its laws. We see how real the risk was in the temporary quarrel which divided Peter and Paul (Gal. 2.11–14). Peter was tempted to 'judaïze' the Church, to restrict it within the practices of the law and to impose these on the Gentiles who were being converted. Those with James did the same and Barnabas let himself be carried along with them. So Paul was called by Christ to be sent 'far away to the Gentiles' (Acts 22.21), to stop the judaïzing tendency which the twelve risked, to defend the universality of the Church, where Jews and Gentiles could enter without one having to submit to the other, being equal before God's grace. This addition of Paul to the twelve is a warning to the Church which will at times have to admit that prophetic events may come to judge the apostolic institution , when it comes up against the dangers of rigidity and lack of faithfulness to the Holy Spirit. In short, the choice of Paul as an apostle of Christ means that God intended the apostolate to be extended. Of course the college of the twleve had a precise significance in revealing the Church as the new Israel. The twelve with Paul had a unique apostleship, which was the foundation of the Church in the continuing line of Israel and opening it to the whole universe; as such their apostleship could not be passed on. Because it was unique and could not be handed down, the apostleship of the twelve and Paul will always remain present in the Church; these thirteen apostles will never cease ruling the Church through God's word which they passed down and which is recorded in the New Testament. They were the priviliged witnesses of the life, death and resurrection of Christ; they received the promise of the inspiration of the Holy Spirit to transmit God's word to the Church, both directly, by speaking or writing themselves, and indirectly, in the speaking and writing of their immediate disciples. But

Christ desired that they should hand over a part of their apostleship, which could be passed on in their ministry as founders and leaders of Churches, so that the Church might be established in the whole world by the preaching of the Gospel. The choice of Paul as Christ's thirteenth apostle was a breach in the institution of the twelve made by God himself, so as to show Christ's apostles that they had to grow in number, creating apostles in their turn. Christ's thirteen apostles could and had to institute apostles of apostles, apostles 'through men' (Gal. 1.1). Christ in glory would no longer choose apostles directly; Paul was the last; but his choice, which opened up the college of the twelve, was Christ's invitation to the apostles to hand over a part of their apostleship to disciples who would become their helpers and delegates in founding and ruling Churches. The extension of the Church demanded this extension of apostleship. Of course, in the instititution of the seven (Acts 6.1–7), in the presbyteral organisation of the Church, the apostles had understood that they had to be helped by ministers. But with the choice of Paul, Christ invited them to extend the ministry of apostleship itself: in the Church there would not only be presbyters and deacons, assistants to Christ's apostles, but also apostles of apostles, the apostles' helpers and delegates, with the apostolic mission to found and rule over Churches, with the ecumenical function of linking Churches together in unity, in communion with the twelve and Paul. With Paul's ministry among the Gentiles the geographical extension of the Church demanded this extension of the apostolate.

4

THE FELLOW WORKERS
OF THE APOSTLES

It was in this way that after the twelve, who were chosen during the Son of God's life on earth, and after Matthias and Paul, who were chosen by Christ himself in glory, without any human intermediary, a third category of apostles came into being: the apostles of apostles, apostles' helpers and delegates. They were not successors to the apostles in the true sense. The idea of a succession of apostles could not have existed in the mind of the infant Church; because of God's secrecy on Christ's second coming, the apostles thought they would live to see his return. They could not have intended to create any successors because they were awaiting the Lord's imminent return. That intention could have come later when they realized they were near to death. But, quite soon after the beginning of their mission, the apostles needed delegated helpers and fellow workers locally, because of the geographical extension of the Church. They instituted on the one hand apostles who were helpers or delegates to ensure with them the foundation and government of new Churches and the ecumenical link between them, and on the other hand presbyters and bishops to preside over the local Churches.

St Paul's epistles refer to this first instititution of apostolic fellow workers: auxiliary apostles, apostolic delegates, missionaries and evangelists.[8]

There are firstly those who are explicitly given the title of apostle in the New Testament, but were not named 'by Jesus Christ and God the Father, who raised him from the dead' (Gal. 1.1). Admittedly their inner vocation was supernatural and came from God, but they were not chosen by an outward manifestation of Christ, like the twelve called by Jesus at the time of his incarnation, Matthias chosen by divine lot and Paul caught up in an appearance of the risen Lord. It was the apostles of Christ themselves who recognized them and instituted them apostles of apostles. It was through the intermediary of the apostles or an apostle, 'from men or through man' (Gal. 1.1), that they received outward confirmation of their inner vocation.

Barnabas was one of those apostles. First he played an important role in presenting the converted Paul to the Church at Jerusalem which was afraid of him; he took him to the apostles and told them about the conversion of the new apostle chosen by Christ (Acts 9.27). He is decribed as a good man, full of the Holy Spirit and of faith (Acts 11.24). He was sent by the Church at Jerusalem to Antioch to encourage that newly founded Church (Acts 11.22–23); then he took the initiative in going to look for Paul at Tarsus to bring him to Antioch; they ministered together in that Church for a year (Acts 11.25–26). They were both sent to Jerusalem to help the Christians of Judea (Acts 11.30). Later we find Barnabas again at Antioch, named first among the five prophets and teachers who were ministering in the Church; Paul is named last (Acts 13.1). At a time of fasting and worshipping the Holy Spirit ordered the five to set apart Barnabas and Saul for an itinerant mission. They laid hands on them and they set off on their mission (Acts 13.2–3). Again Barnabas is named first, as later when they are at Paphos. However, in the course of the story Paul is several times named first. Yet at Lystra Barnabas once again seems to take first place; he is taken for Zeus and Paul for Hermes 'because he was the chief speaker' (Acts 14.12). All this in any case indicates equality in apostleship ('the apostles Barnabas and Paul', Acts 14.14). At last, having worked together for a long time, Paul and Barnabas part company. So here we see Barnabas and Paul freely accepting their responsibilities as equals, with neither being above the other. Barnabas is wholly an apostle, with the ministry and authority that that implies. He is an apostle 'through men', but his apostleship is no less recognized as coming from Christ: he has authority and responsibility equal to that of Paul.

Thus in the ministry of Matthias and Paul we see growing up in the early Church an apostolic ministry which does not originate from Christ in his humanity, like that of the twelve. It is an apostolic ministry given by the Holy Spirit, integrated into the ministry of the first apostles and recognized by the Church. These new apostles were imposed on the Church by the Holy Spirit. These apostles had to show the genuine fruits of the ministry that they received from the Holy Spirit; St Paul strongly criticizes the ministry of 'false apostles' who disturbed rather than built up the Church at Corinth (2 Cor. 11–13). They called themselves apostles out of pride. Paul calls them 'superlative apostles', not allowing them any true authority in the Church (2 Cor. 11.5). Paul is not attacking the fact that there were new apostles, but rather the pride of the 'false apostles', the 'superlative apostles'. The Book of Revelation also refers to 'those who call themselves apostles but are not, and [you] found them to be false' (Rev. 2.2).

Among those who are rightly called apostles we find further Silas or Silvanus and Timothy. Silvanus and Timothy are Paul's fellow workers on several missionary journeys and Paul, writing to the Thessalonians, adds their names to his in the salutation (1 Thess. 1.1; 2 Thess. 1.1). In the course of the first letter he refers to them explicitly as apostles: '... though we might have made demands as apostles of Christ' (1 Thess. 2.6). Epaphroditus was also among these apostles added to the early college: 'I have thought it necessary to send to you Epaphroditus my brother and fellow worker and fellow soldier (sunergos, sustratiotes), and your messenger and minister to my need' (Phil. 2.25). If the name apostle is to be taken here in the sense of 'messenger' from the church at Philippi, the titles sunergos (fellow worker) and sustratiotes (fellow soldier) are a good indication of the role of these second generation apostles who are Paul's missionary companions. If the initial college of apostles was created by Christ with the apostles who witnessed his resurrection, it is increased in the next stage by the apostles' companions who share their work and their struggle in mission and in founding Churches. These new apostles, raised up by the Holy Spirit in the Church, fellow workers and fellow combatants of the first apostles of Christ, are essentially missionaries and founders. It is by virtue of this that they are also called apostles. They are apostles of apostles;[9] they share with the first apostles the responsibility of mission, of founding and supervising Churches. They are the apostles' companions in service (*sundoulos*), like Epaphras, of whom Paul writes to the Colossians: 'a servant of Christ Jesus... always remembering you earnestly in his prayers, that you may stand mature and fully assured in all the will of God. For I bear witness that he has worked hard for you and for those in Laodicea and in Hierapolis' (Col. 4.12–13). Paul calls him his fellow servant (*sundoulos*, Col. 1.7), and so we see him sharing with him the care of the Churches.

The word 'evangelist', used three times in the New Testament, probably also indicates these second generation apostles. Philip, one of the seven ordained by the apostles, is given this title (Acts 21.8). In the Epistle to the Ephesians (4.11) St. Paul quotes the beginning of the list of ministries instituted by God himself in the Church:

apostles, prophets,
evangelists, pastors and teachers.

There is an order to this enumeration: apostles and evangelists share a ministry of an itinerant nature, of mission and foundation; prophets and pastors and teachers have a ministry of a stable nature, of building and continuation. Moreover the apostles and prophets belong to the first generation of the Church: they are the first founders and builders of the Church. 'You are fellow citizens with the saints and members of the household of God', writes St Paul, 'built upon the foundation of the apostles and prophets' (Eph. 2.19–20); the apostles are the first missionaries-founders, the prophets are the first preachers-builders. The evangelists appear as the first apostles' helpers in mission and in founding Churches; the pastors-teachers are successors to the prophets in preaching and teaching and in building up local Churches. 'Do the work of an evangelist', writes Paul to Timothy (2 Tim. 4.5); the latter had been associated with Paul in an apostleship of mission and foundation.

Thus we see the initial apostolic college develop; for the ministry of mission, of foundation and of supervision was necessarily extended according to the demands of the growing Church.

When we think of episcopal ministry in the Church, in the succession of apostolic ministry, we should remember this first period of the extension of the college of the twelve and the motives behind it. The college of apostles was increased by apostles of apostles, by evangelists or apostolic delegates in proportion to the growing demands of mission, foundation and supervision. The apostles' first helpers were missionaries, founders and itinerant overseers. This shows us the essential and basic nature of episcopacy in the Church: throughout its history, according to its needs, bishops were given to the Church by the Holy Spirit, admitted to the initial college of apostles, to become evangelists, fellow workers, fellow combatants and fellow servants to the first apostles, missionaries, founders and coordinators.

If the initial apostolic college was increased by new apostles, apostolic fellow workers or evangelists, so ministry in the local Church developed accordingly.

In St Luke's Gospel there is reference to two missions, that of the twelve and that of the seventy (or, according to some manuscripts, seventy-two: Luke 9.1–6, 10.1–16). In the accounts of these two missions, most elements are common to the twelve apostles and to the seventy disciples: they are all ordered to proclaim the kingdom of God, to heal the sick and to shake the dust from their feet as a sign of judgement if they are not received.

The number seventy is probably deliberate.[10] Just as the twelve are the patriarchs of the new Israel, so the seventy represent the elders of Israel, gathered together by Moses at God's command: 'Gather for me seventy men of the elders of Israel, whom you know to be the elders of the people and officers over them; and bring them to the tent of meeting, and let them take their stand there with you. And I will come down and talk with you there; and I will take some of the spirit which is upon you and put it upon them; and they shall bear the burden of the people with you, that you may not bear it yourself alone' (Num. 11.16–17). So Moses gathered the seventy elders who received the spirit and began to prophesy. Another detail in the story strengthens the parallel between the seventy elders of Israel and the seventy disciples of Christ. There is in fact a reference to two other elders who did not come to the gathering and began to prophesy in the camp. Moses rejoiced and wished that all the people were prophets. These two extra elders, Eldad and Medad, brought the number of elders to seventy-two (Num. 11.24–30). Now some manuscripts of Luke's Gospel refer to seventy-two disciples. Perhaps that is an attempt to make the two passages appear to coincide.[11]

If the seventy were designated by Christ like the elders by Moses it was indeed to bear the burden of the people with Christ and with the twelve. If the Spirit had come upon the seventy elders, the seventy disciples were designated by the Lord himself; they received the task of proclaiming God's kingdom, healing the sick and treading underfoot any power of the enemy (Luke 10.19); whoever heard them heard Christ himself, so whoever rejected them rejected the Father who had sent him (Luke 10.16). They were to rejoice that their names were written in heaven rather than because spirits were subject to them. They were truly marked by God for that ministry and that mission, as the seventy elders had been clad in the Spirit to bear the burden of the people with Moses and to prophesy.[12]

Thus ministry did not all flow from just the college of the twelve by extension and succession. Ministry came from Christ and took shape first in the college of the twelve, then in the group of seventy, first in the apostles, then in the prophets. 'You are', wrote Paul, 'built upon the foundation of the apostles and prophets, Christ Jesus himself being the corner-stone' (Eph. 2.20).

Thus when the apostles were establishing local ministries, for the needs of local churches, they did not delegate in its entirety the ministry they had received, but they acted like Moses: they chose elders who shared their office among God's people and received the Holy Spirit to preach God's word and to prophesy; they acted like Christ: they sent out disciples to announce the coming of the kingdom.

For St Luke, ministry from its first institution by Christ, divides into two groups: that of the twelve apostles, patriarchs of the new Israel, and that of the seventy disciples, elders and prophets of the new Israel. In the infant Church we see the same division continuing and changing: the apostles and their helpers, on the one hand, who founded and governed Chruches, and on the other hand local ministries, which built up and ruled over a local church.

Admittedly in Christ's institution of ministries, the seventy appear above all to be itinerant, like the apostles. Yet Luke's definite reference to the seventy elders and scribes around Moses allowed the infant Church to see in them the origin of its prophets, pastors and teachers. Besides, the local ministry of the early Church was still to be a missionary one.

The first apostolic act instituting a local ministry was the choice of the seven at Jerusalem. Because of the complaint by the Hellenists (Greek-speaking Jews who had become Christians), who felt neglected by comparison with the Hebrews, the apostles suggested that the Church choose 'seven men of good repute, full of the Spirit and of wisdom' to serve tables at the agape. The apostles could not carry out every task, they had to devote themselves above all to 'prayer and to the ministry of the word' (Acts 6.1–6). After the assembly had made its choice, the apostles nominated the seven to this particular service of the agape; they were brought before the apostles who, after prayer, laid hands on them. It is not accurate to see in these seven what the Church was later to call deacons.[13] Admittedly they were ordained in the first place for this ministry of the agape, but two of them were revealed as having fuller gifts: Stephen appeared as a prophet (preacher), 'a man full of faith and of the Holy Spirit… full of grace and power, doing great wonders and signs among the people' (Acts 6.5–8); and Philip as an evangelist (a missionary and apostle's helper, Acts 21.8), who preached, taught, baptized and performed miracles of healing (Acts 8. 5–8, 12–13, 26–40).

This ordination of the seven, the local ministers at Jerusalem, corresponds to a tradition of the Synagogue. According to Jewish tradition a community of 120 men was entitled to elect a local sanhedrin of seven elders. So the seven appeared as seven presbyters (elders) who were to assist the apostles at Jerusalem.

From 38 AD we see James the brother of Jesus taking the role of president in the Church at Jerusalem. When the converted Paul went up to Jerusalem he visited Peter, the chief of the apostles, and James the head of the local church at Jerusalem (Gal. 1.19). James may first have headed a group of Jewish Hebrew-speaking Christians, but from the manuscripts his authority seems to have been extended to all the Christians at Jerusalem. After being freed from prison Peter asked that the news be sent 'to James and to the brethren' (Acts 12.17).

At the time of the dispute at Antioch about the converted Gentiles (did they have to observe the law to be saved?), Paul and Barnabas were sent to Jerusalem to put the case to the apostles and the presbyters. When they arrived at Jerusalem they were received by the Church, the apostles (Peter and John: Gal. 2.9) and the elders, led by James, who met to examine the problem. After a long discussion Peter spoke first, then Barnabas and Paul related everything God had done among the Gentiles. Finally James spoke and delivered the solution with authority, a solution which was repeated in the letter from the apostles and elders sent to the Church at Antioch. The way in which James speaks, after the apostles Peter, John, Barnabas and Paul, shows that he enjoyed the authority of a leader at Jerusalem. 'Therefore my judgement is that we should not trouble those of the Gentiles who turn to God... ' (Acts 15.19). The decision was to be taken by 'the apostles and elders with the whole church' to send Judas and Silas to Antioch, with Paul and Barnabas, with a letter from the apostles and elders (Acts 15.22–23). The letter used the solemn words: 'It has seemed good to the Holy Spirit and to us...' (Acts 15.28). When St Paul recounted the incident he wrote: 'James and Cephas and John, who were reputed to be pillars, gave to me and Barnabas the right hand of fellowship' (Gal. 2.9). Here James is named first, as head of the Church at Jerusalem, which underlines his important local authority.[14]

These passages show us the presence of certain apostles of universal authority at Jerusalem, and a college of presbyters headed by James the brother of Jesus. The authority of the apostles at Jerusalem was extended to all the Churches; they shared their authority with other apostles, like Paul and Barnabas, according to their different missions: 'He who worked through Peter for the mission to the circumcised', wrote Paul, 'worked through me also for the Gentiles' (Gal. 2.8). Peter and John were sent to Samaria to bring the Samaritans into the Church through the laying on of hands (Acts 8.14–17). But the apostles' universal ministry did not preclude a local ministry; on the contrary, we see the authority of James clearly manifested at Jerusalem, assisted by the elders, including the seven (except Stephen the martyr) who were set aside especially for service to the Hellenists. Despite his universal authority and his leadership among the twelve, Peter did not usurp the local authority of James, who played an important role at Jerusalem. It was the same for Paul, whom we see much later received again at Jerusalem by James, when all the elders were present (Acts. 21.18). It was they who advised Paul to take part in a liturgical act to appease the Jews.

The structure of the church at Jerusalem followed Jewish tradition: the synagogue was made up of a college of elders presided over by a 'head of the synagogue'. Jerusalem was probably divided into various Christian groups; in any case we know of the Hebrews and the Hellenists who brought into the church what had distinguished them in various synagogues: Hebrew or Greek language and culture (Acts 6.1). The elders, under the leadership of James, had to represent these different congregations in a presbyteral college, which ensured authority and unity in the church at Jerusalem. The apostles at Jerusalem continued to carry out their ministry of speaking and praying, enjoying the apostolic authority which extended to all the Churches. These two bodies of ministries seem to function in perfect harmony and mutual respect: the apostolic body, with its universal authority, its various missions, those of Peter and Paul and the college of elders led by James. The apostolic body had greater mobility, because of Christ's command to found and rule over Churches in the world; the apostles would move around, laying foundations and visiting. The body of elders, in accordance with its synagogical origin was a local and stable college, with a single head.

Outside Jerusalem, wherever the Church took root in the Jewish synagogue, this structure of presbyters from the local community can be seen to appear, with the college of elders bringing together the various ministries of prophets, pastors and teachers, ensuring the smooth running of the church, its authority and unity in charity.

When a local church was founded among the Gentiles these ministers were given the name of *episkopes*, overseers.[15] These overseers were the equivalent of elders; they were helped in their ministry by deacons. Thus at the beginning of the Epistle to the Philippians we read: 'Paul and Timothy... to all the saints in Christ Jesus who are at Philippi, with the bishops and deacons...' (Phil. 1.1). The saints (or faithful) of Philippi were governed by a college of bishops (or overseers) and deacons (or servants) who made secure the ministry in the Church.[16]

So it seems that, whatever the names given to various ministers, the organization of ministries was always done on a collegiate basis, not excluding leadership of the college of ministers, which was either alternating or permanent.

At Jerusalem, at least, this leadership of the college seems to have been fixed. James was the permanent head of the college of elders and of the community. Gradually this form came to be imposed on the whole Church, whose ministries were to be organized into a college of elders headed by an overseer, the bishop of the early Church.[17]

5

THE APOSTLES' SUCCESSORS

While the ministries in the local church were being organised into a college of elders with a leader, the ministry of the apostles and their helpers was continuing and ensuring a link between all the Churches. This universal apostolic ministry still remained valid and necessary so that the local churches did not lose contact and true communion in the unity of the faith, of sacraments and of ministries. As the apostles began to grow old and feel death was near, there arose the problem of their succession, or at least the problem of a succession to their universal apostolic ministry, which was indispensable if the unity of local churches was to be maintained. At the beginning of their ministry they might have believed that Christ's return was imminent and had not thought about a succession in the apostolic ministry, a ministry of foundation, of government and of unity.

This second stage comes out clearly in the so-called Pastoral Epistles, to Timothy and Titus. For our purposes it is not important to establish whether they were written by Paul or one of his disciples on the basis of the apostle's notes. Either way they are the spiritual testament of an apostle who wished to see his ministry continued despite his death.[18]

The apostle felt that his end was near: 'For I am already on the point of being sacrificed; the time of my departure has come. I have fought the good fight, I have finished the race, I have kept the faith' (2 Tim. 4.6–7). He saw the crown of justice that the Lord would give him on the great day, as he would to all those who in love had awaited his appearance. He might have thought that before dying he would see that appearance, that glorious day of Christ's return, but now he felt that death was near, the fight ended and the race over; and he would have to await Christ's appearance elsewhere. All the time he expected the Lord's return in his own lifetime the problem of the succession to the apostleship did not arise; it was enough to extend its activity thanks to fellow workers, companions in service and in the fight. But now that he felt death was appraoching he had to think of the next stage in his apostolic ministry, which was necessary for the unity of the Churches, for the faithful maintaining of the faith, for the foundation and building of new Churches, and for the organization of ministries for training God's people.

Out of his fellow workers, his companions in service and in the fight, he was to make successors in the apostolic ministry. Timothy and Titus were among them. These men of God (1 Tim. 6.11) he called his children or his sons. They were to inherit from their father in the apostolate the ministry of government necessary for the unity of Churches: 'To Timothy, my beloved child ... You then, my son, be strong in the grace ... To Titus, my true child in a common faith...' (1 Tim. 1.2, 18; 2 Tim. 1.2; 2.1; Titus 1.4). This affectionate, paternal name of 'son' underlines the link uniting the apostle to his successors. He left them his spiritual testament, so that they might replace him faithfully in the apostolate, as true sons who continue their father's work.

A careful reading of the three epistles which form this spiritual testament shows us how Timothy, for the Church at Ephesus, and Titus for the Church at Crete, could become what Paul had been for the Churches in the apostolic ministry. They to be firstly *imitators of the apostle*: they were his sons, so they had to conform to what they saw in him to become what he had been for all the Churches. Further, they had to become custodians of the apostolic faith. Finally they had to take on the duty of being *organizers of the ministry*.

The apostle's successor must be firstly his imitator; he must imitate him in *his faith and charity* (1 Tim. 1.12–17), in *his fight and suffering* in the cause of the Gospel (2 Tim. 1.8–12; 2.3–10); thus, like the apostle, he will be a stimulating *example* to the faithful and to the ministers of the Church in his care. Paul writes: 'But I received mercy for this reason, that in me, as the foremost, Jesus Christ might display his perfect patience for an example to those who were to believe in him for eternal life... Follow the pattern of the sound words which you have heard from me, in the faith and love which are in Christ Jesus... Share in suffering for the Gospel... Share in suffering as a good soldier of Christ Jesus... Set the believers an example in speech and conduct, in love, in faith, in purity... Show yourself in all respects a model of good deeds, and in your teaching show integrity, gravity, and sound speech that cannot be censured, so that an opponent may be put to shame, having nothing evil to say of us' (1 Tim. 1.16; 2 Tim. 1.13, 8; 2.3; 1 Tim. 4.12; Titus 2.7–8).

It is important to note this first demand made on Paul's successor. It is not automatic, because he has been designated by the apostle or by sacramental grace. Timothy and Titus are successors to the apostle by virtue of their faith and charity which conform to those of the apostle, because they are ready to fight and suffer like him for the Gospel, because, imitating him, they can be living examples among the ministers and the faithful for whom they are responsible before God. In the three letters Paul begins by insisting on his successor's faith: 'To Timothy, my true child in the faith... The aim of our charge is love that issues from a pure heart and a good conscience and sincere faith... I am reminded of your sincere faith... To Titus, my true child in a common faith...' (1 Tim. 1.2,5; 2 Tim 1.5; Titus 1.4). Thus it is through faith that the succession is bound to the apostle, like a father to his son, a deep faith that creates unity in knowledge and the confession of truth, in charity, fighting and suffering for the Gospel. In the inward imitation of the apostle's faith, the successor may in his turn be a living example in the Church.

In imitation of the apostle, his successor was to be the guardian of the apostolic faith which he professed with the apostle. The final charge to Timothy which sums up the whole of the first letter is precisely this: 'O Timothy, guard what has been entrusted to you' (1 Tim. 6.20). Paul, who felt death approaching, knew by faith that God would preserve his teaching until Christ's return, and at the same time he exhorted his successor to be submissive to the Holy Spirit in guarding what had been entrusted to him: 'I know whom I have believed and I am sure that he is able to guard until that Day what has been entrusted to me. Follow the pattern of the sound words which you have heard from me, in the faith and love which are in Christ Jesus; guard the truth that has been entrusted to you by the Holy Spirit who dwells within us' (2 Tim. 1.12–14).

What was entrusted to him was the whole Gospel that he received through the apostles, by the personal revelation of the risen Christ, and by the inspiration of the Holy Spirit who led him into complete truth. It included the teaching of the fundamental truths of the Christian faith, the tradition of sacraments and of prayer according to Christ's word, the instititution of the Christian community in charity and unity and the order of ministries in the service of the priestly people of the Church. It was the whole of this apostolic teaching that the apostle passed on to the Churches and which he upheld in them through his visits and letters. The apostle knew that his Lord, in his might, would keep this gospel intact until his return in glory. Even if the apostle had to be taken away from the Church on earth the faith which he had carefully guarded could not deteriorate or perish; it was too precious: God would act that it might be kept. Even if false doctrines were to come and obstruct the truth, that which was entrusted to the apostles would be preserved by God in the Church. Indeed, man's infidelity is powerless before the faithfulness of God (2 Tim. 2.13).

The apostle also entrusts this apostolic confession of faith, which he is sure the Lord will preserve until Christ's return, to his successor: the latter must, through his ministry, become an instrument in God's hands to guard the apostolic treasure: 'Guard the truth that has been entrusted to you by the Holy Spirit who dwells within us' (2 Tim. 1.14). No less than the apostle, his successor has no power of himself to guard the truth which is entrusted to him; it is solely 'by the Holy Spirit' that he can fulfil this ministry. The apostle may depart in peace: he has faith in his Lord to keep the Gospel by the Holy Spirit which will indwell his successor and act in his ministry.

Several times the apostle insists on the purity of the doctrine that his successor must guard and pass on; it is 'the faith of God's elect and their knowledge of the truth which accords with godliness, in hope of eternal life' (Titus 1.1–2). The minister succeeding the apostle must watch over this faith of God's elect and this knowledge of the truth which produces godliness and guides hope. 'If you put these instructions before the brethren', writes Paul to his successor, 'you will be a good minister of Christ Jesus, nourished on the words of the faith and of the good doctrine which you have always followed... Take heed to yourself and to your teaching; hold to that, for by so doing you will save both yourself and your hearers' (1 Tim. 4.6,16). The word *didaskalia*, which means 'doctrinal teaching', occurs fifteen times in the three epistles to Timothy and Titus (1 Tim. 1.10; 4.1,6,13,16; 5.17; 6.1,3: 2 Tim. 3.10, 16; 4.3; Titus 1.9; 2.1, 7,10); once with the pejorative meaning of 'doctrines of demons' (1 Tim. 4.1). Elsewhere in the New Testament we find the word only six times, of which four have the pejorative meaning of 'human doctrines' (the only two positive uses are in Rom. 12.7 and 15.4). This is indicative of the originality and importance of this idea in the Pastoral Epistles.

At the same time another theme should be noted which occurs nine times in different forms: the *sound* nature of doctrine, words and faith (1 Tim. 1.10; 6.3; 2 Tim. 1.13; 4.3; Titus 1.9,13; 2.1,2,8). The apostle attaches key importance to his successor maintaining a sound doctrine so that he may teach in accordance with truth: 'As for you', he writes to Titus, 'teach what befits sound doctrine' (Titus 2.1). The apostle knows from experience the dangers for the Christian faith of unsound doctrinal teaching: 'The Spirit expressly says that in later times some will depart from the faith by giving heed to deceitful spirits and doctrines of demons, through the pretensions of liars whose consciences are seared' (1 Tim. 4.1–2). Several times in these epistles, the apostle warns his successor against false doctrines which corrupt the faith. As the guardian of sound doctrine and in proclaiming a sound message to nourish a sound faith, the apostle's successor must also be the judge of those who oppose that doctrine by their bad teaching: 'Remain at Ephesus', Paul writes to Timothy, 'that you may charge certain persons not to teach any different doctrine, nor to occupy themselves with myths and endless genealogies which promote speculations rather than the divine training that is in faith' (1 Tim. 1.3–4). The apostle sees these false teachers especially among the judaïzers: 'For there are many insubordinate men, empty talkers and deceivers, especially the circumcision party' (Titus 1.10). But there would be others, and the apostle's successor must be vigilant in order to make judgements on the basis of the sound doctrine which nourishes faith and maintains unity. False teachers create factions and divisions; the apostle's successor must at times use severity to keep the faithful in faith and unity: 'As for a man who is factious (a "heretical" man), after admonishing him once or twice, have nothing more to do with him' (Titus 3.10).

Several times Paul gives short summaries of the doctrine, like brief symbols of faith, some in the form of hymns which probably belonged to the liturgy of the Church, which were part of what was entrusted to him, and which could remind the apostle's successor how he should teach the faith (1 Tim. 6.15–16; 2.5; 3.16; 2 Tim. 2.11–13; Titus 2.11–14; 3.4–7).

However precise and demanding these doctrinal statements by the apostle may be, they do not form a rational theological apologetic, a fighting doctrine. Admittedly the apostle and his successor had to take a stand against corruptions of the Gospel, but the best way for them to keep what was entrusted to them was to express it in the form of praise to the one God and the one mediator between God and men (1 Tim. 2.5). Christian theology is an expression of adoration, the doctrine to be taught is a form of contemplation, the dogma is liturgical doxology. This theology of praise, which constituted the faith, was the entire dogmatics of the early Church. For the apostle doctrine and godliness are indissolubly linked: from sound doctrine there emerges true godliness. If the 'doctrine' (*didaskalia*) is peculiar to the Pastoral Epistles, where we find it so frequently, it is the same with the word 'godliness' or 'piety' (*eusebeia*)[19]; it is found ten times in these three epistles, out of fifteen occurrences in the New Testament (once in Acts 3.12 and four times in 2 Pet. 1.3,6,7; 3.11); it should be added that the adverb *eusebos*, 'with godliness', is found only twice in the New Testament, and precisely in these Pastoral Epistles (2 Tim. 3.12; Titus 2.12: [RSV 'live a godly life']). To be a faithful guardian of the faith entrusted to him the apostle's successor must bring the exercise of godliness to doctrinal faithfulness: 'While bodily training is of some value, godliness is of value in every way, as it holds promise for the present life and also for the life to come' (1 Tim. 4.8). If Timothy is thus exhorted to train himself in godliness, it is because he will only be able to stand in the sound doctrine, guard what is entrusted to him and transmit it, if he is a man of prayer and contemplation, a man of God: 'But as for you, man of God, shun all this (the behaviour of a false teacher); aim at righteousness, godliness, faith, love, steadfastness, gentleness. Fight the good fight of the faith...' (1 Tim. 6.11–12). Indeed, the false minister of Christ 'does not agree with the sound words of our Lord Jesus Christ and the teaching which accords with godliness' (1 Tim. 6.3). The apostle's successor, as Christ's faithful minister, agrees, on the contrary, with the word of the Lord and with the doctrine which is formed in godliness and which stimulates godliness. The faith of God's elect and the knowledge of truth accords with godliness in the hope of eternal life (Titus 1.1–2). Doctrine and godliness are so closely linked that the apostle can even use one word in place of the other: 'Great indeed is the mystery of our godliness' (1 Tim. 3.16, Authorised Version). Here we are concerned with the fundamental content of the apostolic doctrine and also of Christian godliness: the mystery of the incarnate Christ, justified, contemplated, proclaimed, believed and raised up in glory.

This sound doctrine, which accords with godliness, inspired by the words of Christ and the faith of the apostles, constitutes the faith which the apostle's successor must transmit: 'Now you have observed my teaching, my conduct, my aim in life, my faith, my patience, my love, my steadfastness, my persecutions, my sufferings... As for you, continue in what you have learned and have firmly believed, knowing from whom you have learned it and how from childhood you have been acquainted with the sacred writings which are able to instruct you for salvation through faith in Christ Jesus. All scripture is inspired by God and profitable for teaching, for reproof, for correction, and for training in righteousness, that the man of God may be complete, equipped for every good work' (2 Tim. 3.10–11,14–17). Timothy had received the whole tradition of the Christian faith through the Scripture and apostolic teaching. He had followed the apostle in everything as a father in the faith. Thus he was well-equipped for a good ministry as a successor to the apostle. But he could not keep for himself what he had learnt in this way; he had to transmit it in turn to others. He was a link in the chain transmitting the faith; this was transmitted first by Christ to the apostles, then by the apostles to their helpers, their fellow workers and then their successors; the apostles' successors in their turn had to transmit in a faithful tradition that good thing entrusted to them by the apostles.

'You then, my son', Paul wrote to Timothy, 'be strong in the grace that is in Christ Jesus, and what you have heard from me before many witnesses entrust to faithful men who will be able to teach others also' (2 Tim. 2.1–2). The idea of tradition, as transmission of the apostolic faith, is summed up here. The apostle's successor must seek all the strength of his ministry in the grace of Christ; all that he had heard from the apostle, as a son from his father, either directly or through the intermediary of faithful witnesses, the apostolic Gospel, sound doctrine according with godliness, all this consigned to his keeping he must in turn commit to the charge (*paratheke*: a trust, deposit; *parathou*: commit to the charge) of *faithful men*, who would be capable of transmitting this sound apostolic teaching to others. Thus the apostle's faith must be kept intact by his successor, to be transmitted faithfully, in accordance with authentic tradition, to reliable, able men who would continue this transmission, this tradition in the Church. In this reference to faithful, able men (*pistoi, hikanoi*) we have in embryo the whole organization of the ministry of the apostle's successor. Timothy, who is the custodian of the faith, and will transmit it to faithful, able men, thus organizes the ministry.

Timothy holds from God this duty of succeeding the apostle, of guarding the faith and organizing the ministry, by vocation and ordination, even though God used Paul to call and direct him. The apostle himself reminds Timothy of this future vocation and this early preparation: 'I am reminded of your sincere faith, a faith that dwelt first in your grandmother Lois and your mother Eunice and now, I am sure, dwells in you' (2 Tim. 1.5), 'From childhood you have been acquainted with the sacred writings' (3.15), Timothy was the son of a Greek and a Jewess who was probably converted to Christianity after the first visit of Paul and Barnabas to Lystra: 'He (Timothy) was well spoken of by the brethren at Lystra and Iconium' (Acts 16.2). At the time of his second journey Paul met him at Lystra and decided to take him with him; henceforth Timothy was to stay with him as one of his most faithful helpers.

God himself chose Timothy for the ministry, through the intermediary of Paul. His vocation was confirmed by the Church in his ordination. The apostle reminds him of that ordination, by which he received God's *charisma*, the gift of the Holy Spirit, with a view of ministry, and by ordination too this gift and ministry were recognized, accepted and confirmed by the Church: 'Do not neglect the gift you have (the gift of the Spirit), which was given you by prophetic utterance when the council of elders laid their hands on you... I remind you to rekindle the gift of God that is within you through the laying on of my hands; for God did not give us a spirit of timidity but a spirit of power and love and self-control' (1 Tim. 4.14; 2 Tim. 1.6–7).

The ordination of the apostle's fellow worker was thus the act of the Holy Spirit expressed in prophecy, the witness of God and of the Church, and working in a sacramental action, the laying on of hands. So this apostolic ministry is not just the object of the apostle's choice or a tacit or explicit election by the Christian community. Admittedly later in the Church many ways of designating ministers would be accepted. But there would always be times when the apostolic ministry would be overshadowed by the all-powerfulness of choice and consecration by God himself: in prophecy and the laying on of hands. There the Church would act only as the obedient instrument of the Holy Spirit.

Prophecy is the act of God's word being expressed through the ministers of the Church to show that a member of God's people has been added to the ministerial body of the universal Christian community. The laying on of hands is the ecclesial and sacramental act by which is attested the gift of the Holy Spirit for ministry. Let us note here in passing, and we shall return to it later, that the early Church did not go back to the sign of anointing to ordain its ministers.[20] Even if, in the course of history, the Christian liturgy was to use anointing in the rite of ordination, it would remain a secondary symbolic element, the real sacramental act being the laying on of hands. If the New Testament talks of anointing in the Spirit it is always in relation to the priesthood of Christ or to the priesthood of the whole people of God. The Christian minister is anointed in that he is united to Christ the priest as a member of God's whole priestly people. The Christian minister is not a successor to the anointed priests of the old covenant; as a minister he does not have a place in the priestly order of Aaron, he is not a *hiereóus*, he is a *presbyteros* endowed with the gift of the Spirit through the laying on of hands, in the apostolic order which is profoundly original, the new creation of Christ.[21] It could be said that the minister is an anointed priest insofar as all members of God's people, all the laity, are priests in communion with Christ the priest, but as a minister he is an elder among his brethren, a *presbyteros*, chosen and given power by the Spirit and the Church for the apostolic ministry, with the gift and authority of the Holy Spirit, received 'by prophetic utterance when the council of elders laid their hands upon you' (1 Tim. 4.14).

6

SUCCESSION IN THE
APOSTOLIC MINISTRY

We have seen how, beginning with Christ, an apostolic ministry was formed in the service of the Church's royal and prophetic priesthood; then how this apostolic college of the twelve around Christ was gradually extended according to the needs and necessities of evangelization and the existence of the Church.

As the apostles felt death approaching they saw the extension of their ministry in terms of the temporal continuation of the Church until Christ returned.

Paul writing to Timothy expresses this premonition of his approaching death and his pressing desire to see his fellow worker who would soon be his successor in part of the Church: 'For I am already on the point of being sacrificed; the time of my departure has come... Do your best to come to me soon... Do your best to come before winter' (2 Tim. 4.6,9,21). An apostle's fellow workers would quite naturally become his successors after his death. Having extended his ministry geographically during his earthly life, they would extend his ministry in time, after his death. So, having left Timothy at Ephesus (1 Tim. 1.3) Paul in his lifetime left Titus in Crete (Titus 1.5) to continue his ministry, to 'amend what was defective and appoint elders in every town' (Titus 1.5) in accordance with apostolic instructions. After his death how could they not continue this task, in fellowship with the apostle who had given them their mission? They were to be the representatives of the dead apostle as they had been of the living one. Indeed, the mission they received from him to organize a local church was to keep its full meaning and would become even more necessary once the apostle had left this world.

The apostles' fellow workers, who became their successors, were to continue in the Churches the tasks they had been given in their apostolic mission: to complete the organization, appoint priests and deacons, guard the faith entrusted to them and inspire teaching, prayer and charity. The organization of the Churches founded by St Paul was based on a college of presbyters. Following the example of the organization of the Jewish synagogue, St Paul appointed as ministers of the Churches priests who were mature, responsible Christians, charged as a group with organizing the community. In this presbyteral college were prophets, pastors or teachers who were serving God's word, like the rabbis (masters) of the Synagogue. In all probability this presbyteral college always had a president, like James at Jerusalem and the *archisynagogos* in the Synagogue.

At Ephesus Paul gave the elders the title of '*episkopes*', overseers or guardians: 'From Miletus he sent to Ephesus and called to him the elders of the Church'. He said to them: 'Take heed to yourselves and to all the flock, in which the Holy Spirit has made you overseers, to care for the Church of God, which he obtained with the blood of his own Son' (Acts 20.17,28). In this passage the divine origin of the ministry of the elders is clearly indicated: they had been appointed by the Holy Spirit; moreover, their ministry is characterized by the double image of the shepherd and of the guardian of a flock, the pastor and overseer.[22]

Peter applies this double image of the shepherd-guardian or the pastor-overseer to Christ himself: 'For you were straying like sheep, but have now returned to the Shepherd and Guardian of your souls' (1 Pet. 2.25). St Peter sees a relation between Christ the pastor-overseer and the ministers of the Church: 'So I exhort the elders among you, as a fellow elder (*sumpresbyteros*) and a witness of the sufferings of Christ as well as a partaker in the glory that is to be revealed. Tend the flock of God that is your charge (exercising the oversight) (*episkopountes*) not by constraint but willingly, not for shameful gain but eagerly, not as domineering over those in your charge but being examples to the flock. And when the chief shepherd is manifested you will obtain the unfading crown of glory' (1 Pet. 5.1–4). The presbyters-pastors tend and oversee the flock of God, as model, loving, obedient servants, in the fellowship of, and participation in, the ministry of Christ the chief shepherd, from whom they will receive their reward and glory at his second coming. In the Acts of the Apostles (20.28) and the Epistle to the Philippians (1.1) the title of overseer, in the plural, is equivalent to that of presbyter: the presbyter is a mature, experienced Christian, an 'elder' in the community, who received his ministry from God and was 'made overseer (guard, guardian) to care for the Church of God' (Acts 20.28); the word 'presbyter' characterizes ministry in terms of experience of the Christian life, the term *episkope* characterizes it in its function of shepherd, pastor, overseer and guardian; the title 'presbyter' emphasizes a state, while *episkope* stresses a function.

In the Epistles to Timothy and Titus the word *episkope* appears only in the singular and seems to indicate a presbyter called to lead a community within a presbyteral college. 'The saying is sure: if any one aspires to the office of *bishop*, he desires a noble task. Now a bishop must be above reproach, the husband of one wife, temperate, sensible, dignified, hospitable, an apt teacher, no drunkard, not violent but gentle, not quarrelsome, and no lover of money. He must manage his own household well, keeping his children submissive and respectful in every way; for if a man does not know how to manage his own household, how can he care for God's church? He must not be a recent convert, or he may be puffed up with conceit and fall into the condemnation of the devil; moreover he must be well thought of by outsiders, or he may fall into reproach and the snare of the devil' (1 Tim. 3.1–7).

The *episkope* is firstly qualified by his noble function, a fine task (*kalon ergon*) to which one may only legitimately aspire subject to certain conditions. The qualities demanded of a bishop can be summed up as follows: balanced in all things, hospitable, capable of teaching, with the gift of governing, and humble in service. These qualities reveal some of the bishop's essential functions. He is the minister of the internal government of the Church: he can only exercise this spiritual function if he is a faithful husband and a wise father in his human existence. This allusion to a father ruling his family facilitates the idea of an episcopal function carried out by *one* man who rules over one Church, even it it is within a college of presbyters. The bishop is also the minister of teaching God's word. He does not rule the Church on his own personal authority, but in the name of another, Christ the shepherd and unseen guardian of souls (1 Pet. 2.25). So it is by the word of God and in accordance with his teaching that he rules God's Church. He is the ambassador and sign of Christ the chief shepherd (1 Pet. 5.4). That is why he must be capable of that evangelistic and apostolic teaching, being entrusted with, and guardian of, the word of God (1 Tim. 6.20). The bishop is the minister of the Church's external affairs: he must be hospitable (*philoxenos*: a friend of strangers), and non-Christians (those from outside) must be able to recognize his human qualities. Here we see that men's reactions also play a part in the choice of God and of the Church. God also speaks through the world to lead the Church in the election of its ministers and particularly in that of the bishop. Ministry is not only concerned with the inner life of the Church, without the world having anything to do with it. The world's opinion has its role in the choice of a bishop, for if God wants him to be a minister of the Church's government and teaching, he wants him also to be the hospitable, courteous and humble servant of all men.

If, in his duties, a bishop lost his humility in service and that moderation in all things he would run the risk of temptation by the devil who, according to biblical thought, tried to usurp the authority of God himself. Here the allusion to the devil suggests that the bishop has a personal function and responsibility which can allow him to rule the Church well according to God's word but can also constitute the temptation to be proud and to usurp power. Here the good opinion of those from outside is a sign of the authenticity of his episcopal ministry, truly lived as a humble service for the benefit of all men, Christian or non-Christian. If he scandalizes outsiders by his pride, it is a sign that he has fallen into the snare of the devil. The world's opinion of a bishop is not only one of the criteria of his election, but also a stimulating reminder to the bishop to remain indeed the humble servant of God's word in the Church and among all men.

In the Epistle to Titus, *episkope* also appears in the singular. Admittedly Paul talks first of the elders whom Titus must appoint in every town in Crete who must fulfil certain spiritual conditions: to have had only one wife, to have children who are believers, and not be profligate or insubordinate (Titus 1.5–6). Then he goes on: 'For a bishop, as God's servant, must be blameless; he must not be arrogant or quick-tempered or a drunkard or violent or greedy for gain, but hospitable, a lover of goodness, master of himself, upright, holy and self-controlled; he must hold firm to the sure word as taught, so that he may be able to give instruction in sound doctrine and also to confute those who contradict it' (Titus 1.7–9). These are the same characteristics of the episcopal office as in the first letter to Timothy. The bishop is God's steward in the Church, he is the administrator of spiritual gifts in God's house; so he must display the qualities needed for that government, complete moderation in all things. He must hold firm to sound teaching; here Paul insists even more on the bishop's teaching ability. The gift of hospitality is essential in his duty of welcoming everyone. So here again the bishop is presented as the minister of the internal government of the Church (*oikonomos*: steward), the minister who guards the faith in the Church, the minister of the Church's external affairs (*philoxenos*: friend of strangers).

In this passage the bishop appears as equivalent to the presbyter. However it is acceptable to suppose that when Paul speaks of presbyters (Titus 1.5–6) he sees in particular their maturity in the Christian life making them suitable for the ministry; when he talks of the bishop (Titus 1.7–9), he underlines, admittedly, the qualities he needs but he sees in particular the function of this minister of government, of doctrine and of welcome.

The Churches founded by Paul and organized by his fellow workers, Timothy and Titus, were headed by a college of presbyters, who probably took it in turns to rule, the president being specially charged with the oversight (*episkope*) which he nonetheless shared with them all. This presbyter became more parcticularly a bishop. This organization corresponds to its antecedents in the Jewish Synagogue and the Church at Jerusalem, with its college of presbyters headed by James. Moreover, this presbyteral-episcopal organization allows us to understand the subsequent development of the Churches.

The letter of St Ignatius to the Ephesians, at the beginning of the second century, confirms the evolution of the ministry at Ephesus and in the other towns of Asia Minor. This evolution can be summarized briefly as follows:

1. Foundation of the Church at Ephesus by Paul, with the institution of a collegiate ministry of presbyters-episcopes on the model of the Synagogue, Paul remaining in overall charge as an apostle (Acts 19.8–10; 20.17–36).

2. Oversight of the Ephesian Church by Timothy, Paul's fellow worker, who had to exhort the bishop, elders, deacons, deaconesses, the widows and all the faithful; the distinction between episcope and presbyter is unclear, if indeed it existed; the ministry is still collegiate.

3. After the successive departures (and the death) of the apostle Paul and of the apostle's fellow worker, Timothy, a presbyter-episcope takes up the responsibility and the oversight of the whole Church at Ephesus; he is the permanent head of the college of presbyters, following the apostle's example, like James at Jerusalem.[23]

4. The letters of St Ignatius to the Ephesians and other neighbouring Churches show the end of this evolution, which took about sixty years; Ignatius talks of the bishop in the college of presbyters, assisted by deacons; the bishop and elders had to be obeyed: they worked in harmony as a lyre with its strings (Ephesians IV; XX).

Thus, from the beginning of the second century, we see a very clear local church structure, the result of the progressive organization of the ministries whose foundations were laid by the apostles.[24]

First and foremost, the bishop who headed the life of the local church, represented Christ, the invisible overseer of the Church; St Ignatius exhorted the Magnesians to respect him, despite his youth, for 'the holy presbyters... have not taken advantage of his outwardly youthful estate, but give place to him as to one prudent in God; yet not to him but to the Father of Jesus Christ, even to the Bishop of all' (Magnesians III). Indeed if we take advantage of the visible bishop, we 'cheat that other who is invisible' (Magn. III). He is not the 'overseer' of the Church because he himself is 'overseen' by God, he submits to the episcopacy of Christ; St Ignatius wrote to Polycarp the 'bishop (overseer) of the church of the Smyrnaeans, or rather who hath for his bishop God the Father and Jesus Christ' (Polycarp, Salutation). He is bishop 'in the flesh', for there is a bishop 'in the spirit' who is Christ. So he is for St. Ignatius the visible sign of Christ the invisible bishop. He is also the sign of the local Church, he represents the community: 'In God's name I have received your whole multitude in the person of Onesimus, whose love passeth utterance and who is moreover your bishop in the flesh', wrote St Ignatius to the Ephesians (I, cf. Magn. II). Since the bishop is the sign of Christ the bishop and of the whole community, the Church may only legitimately come together with him or in fellowship with him: 'Some persons have the bishop's name on their lips but in everything act apart from him. Such men appear to me not to keep a good conscience, forasmuch as they do not assemble themselves together lawfully according to commandment' (Magn. IV). The bishop is a steward of God's house and he is respected by outsiders (Eph. VI, Trallians III). Here we see again the qualities attributed to him in the Pastoral Epistles. As the representative and sign of Christ and of the community, a steward of God's house, he is indeed in the service (*diakonia*) of the Church; St Ignatius wrote to the Philadelphians: 'This your bishop I have found to hold the ministry which pertaineth to the common weal, not of himself, nor through men, nor yet for vain glory, but in the love of God the Father and the Lord Jesus Christ' (Phil. I).

But the bishop is not alone in this divine vocation and ecclesial function, in this representation of God and the Church, this stewardship and this service to the community. He is part of a presbytery; he is united with presbyters and deacons. For St Ignatius this triple order of the ministry is an *objective order* which accords with the mind of Christ (Phil., Salutation), which requires a *moral attitude* of obedience, determines a *canonical spirit* of legitimacy and bears the *spiritual fruit* of unity.

St Ignatius often addresses bishops, presbyters and deacons together: 'I salute your godly bishop and your venerable presbytery and my fellow-servants the deacons' (Smyrnaeans XII). The bishop, presbyters and deacons work together: 'Toil together one with another, struggle together, run together, suffer together, lie down together, rise up together, as God's stewards, and assessors and ministers' (Polycarp VI). In these three functions of steward, assessor and servant, Ignatius indicates the duties proper to the bishop, presbyters and deacons. The bishop is the steward of

God's house, assisted by the presbyters and with the help of the deacons, God's servants. Several comparisons serve as a basis for the *objective order* of the three ministries. 'Be ye zealous to do all things in godly concord, the bishop presiding after the likeness of God and the presbyters after the likeness of the council of the apostles, with the deacons also who are most dear to me, having been entrusted with the diaconate of Jesus Christ' (Magn. VI). And elsewhere: 'Let all men respect the deacons as Jesus Christ, even as they should respect the bishop as being a type of the Father and the presbyters as the council of God and as the college of apostles. Apart from these there is not even the name of a church' (Trallians III). And again: 'Do ye all follow your bishop, as Jesus Christ followed the Father, and the presbytery as the apostles; and to the deacons pay respect as to God's commandment' (Smyr. VIII). In these comparisons the bishop appears as the sign of the authority of God, of the Father or of Christ in the Church; the presbyters represent the authority of God, of the Father or of Christ in the Church; the presbyters represent the authority of the apostles around Christ, joined together in a presbytery, like God's senate, the senate of apostles, the precious spiritual crown (Magn. XIII); the deacons do Christ's service, they are the signs of Christ the servant and are the fellow servants of the bishop.

This objective order founded on Christ and the apostles demands a *moral attitude* of obedience. Addressing Christians Ignatius talks of 'submitting yourselves to your bishop and presbytery (that) ye may be sactified in all things' (Eph. II). The bishop must be regarded 'as the Lord himself' (Eph. VI), and the bishop must not be resisted, 'that by our submission we may give ourselves to God... For every one whom the Master of the household sendeth to be steward over His own house, we ought so to receive Him that sent him' (Eph. V–VI). It should be noted that Ignatius invites obedience to the bishop and presbytery (Eph. XX), because the ministries form a body representing Christ and the apostles. He says of the deacon Zotion that he is 'subject to the bishop as unto the grace of God and to the presbytery as unto the law of Jesus Christ' (Magn. II). To the Trallians he writes: 'Fare ye well in Jesus Christ, submitting yourselves to the bishop as to the commandment and likewise also to the presbytery' (XIII). Thus obedience due to the bishop is due also to the presbytery who surround him, as Christ and the apostles whom they represent are obeyed. It appears that St Ignatius is trying to avoid a monarchical conception of the episcopate, placing it within the college of presbyters. Further, this obedience is not due to men alone, but really to God, his grace and command, for the bishop in the presbytery represents Christ in the midst of the apostles; they are the visible signs of the invisible episcopacy of Christ and of the apostolate of the twelve.

This objective order and moral attitude determine a *canonical situation* of legitimacy. If the bishop and presbyters are the signs of divine and apostolic authority, and if as a result one must submit to them as to the grace and command of the Lord, it is clear that the ecclesial community can only legitimately be assembled in their presence or in fellowship with them, or at least in the presence of the bishop or at his behest. This is true above all for when the community gathers together around the eucharistic table: 'Let no man be deceived. If any one be not within the precinct of the altar, he lacketh the bread of God. For, if the prayer of one and another hath so great force, how much more that of the bishop and of the whole Church. Whosoever therefore cometh not to the congregation, he doth thereby show his pride and hath separated himself' (Eph. V). St Ignatius reminds the Magnesians that they must be united with the bishop and presbyters if there is to be a legitimate assembly of the Church. This union is based on the perfect union of the Son with the Father; 'as the Lord did nothing without the Father, either by Himself or by the apostles, so neither do ye anything without the bishop and the presbyters. And attempt not to think anything right for yourselves apart from others: but let there be one prayer in common, one supplication, one mind, one hope, in love and in joy unblameable, which is Jesus Christ, than whom there is nothing better. Hasten to come together all of you, as to one temple, even God; as to one altar, even to one Jesus Christ, who came forth from One Father and is with One and departed unto One' (VII). Ignatius asks the Trallians to be 'inseparable from (God) Jesus Christ and from the bishop and from the ordinances of the apostles'. He goes on: 'He that is within the sanctuary is clean; but he that is without the sanctuary is not clean, that is, he that doeth ought without the bishop and presbytery and deacons, this man is not clean in his conscience' (VII). To be united inseparably with Jesus Christ 'within the sanctuary', to use Ignatius's image, there must be unity with the bishop, presbytery and deacons. He defines this idea even more carefully in referring to the sacramental life of the Church, which is only legitimate if there is union with the bishop, that is, with Christ, whose presidency and authority he symbolizes, in the midst of the apostolic presbytery and the deacons: 'Do ye all follow your bishop, as Jesus Christ followed the Father, and the presbytery as the apostles; and to the deacons pay respect as to God's commandment. Let no man do aught of things pertaining to the Church apart from the bishop. Let that be held a valid eucharist which is under the bishop or one to whom he shall have committed it. Wheresover the bishop shall appear, there let the people be; even as where Jesus may be, there is the universal Church. It is not lawful apart from the bishop either to baptize or to hold a love-feast; but whatsoever he shall approve, this is well-pleasing also to God; that everything which ye do may be sure and valid' (Smyrn. VIII). Since to follow the bishop is to follow Christ, as he followed the Father, since to follow the presbyterate is to follow the apostles, since deacons must be respected as God's order, it is understandable that nothing can be done in the local Church except in communion with the bishop united with the presbyterate and deacons. The bishop is responsible for the sacraments; the Eucharist, baptism and agape are only valid if he presides or if he delegates another minister for them. It is his approval that makes the sacraments of the Church pleasing to God, sound and valid. Indeed, just as Jesus Christ represents and governs unseen the universal Church ('catholic' appears here for the first time in the tradition), so the bishop represents and presides visibly over the local church.

The objective order of ministries, the obedience it demands and the validity it confers bear in the Church the *spiritual fruit* of unity. The unity of the Church depends on that organic relation of ministries in the service of the gospel and sacraments. St Ignatius takes pleasure in recalling this unity: 'It becometh you to run in harmony with the mind of the bishop; which thing also ye do. For your honourable presbytery, which is worthy of God, is attuned to the bishop, even as its strings to a lyre. Therefore in your concord and harmonious love Jesus Christ is sung. And do ye, each and all, form yourselves into a chorus, that being harmonious in concord and taking the key note of God ye may in unison sing with one voice through Jesus Christ unto the Father, that He may both hear you and acknowledge you by your good deeds to be members of His Son. It is therefore profitable for you to be in blameless unity, that ye may also be partakers of God always' (Eph. IV). The celebration of the Eucharist by the fully united triple ministry is the supreme sign of the unity of the local Church: 'Be ye careful to observe one Eucharist (for there is one flesh of our Lord Jesus Christ and one cup into union in His blood; there is one altar, as there is one bishop, together with the presbytery and the deacons my fellow-servants), that whatsoever ye do, ye may do it after God' (Phil. IV).

The whole subsequent tradition was influenced, in varying ways, by this idea of ministry, which corresponded to an objective order, demanded obedience and conferred validity and bore fruit in unity. These three ministries of the local church, the bishop, presbyterate and deacons, are of a profoundly original character. If they go back to Jewish tradition, the life of the Church gives them a new and particular meaning. There is not a trace of the idea of a sacrificial priesthood, in the sense of the old covenant, in this triple ministry in the service of the gospel, the sacraments and unity. It is a diaconate, a service of Christ, where the minister is the sign of the one whom he serves for the good of the community: the bishop is not the high priest, he is *the sign and instrument* of Christ the high priest and invisible bishop; the college of presbyters places the bishop's authority in a ministerial community: the bishop does not have a monarchical authority, but an authority rooted in *presbyteral collegiality*; finally deacons remind us that ministry is not a power but *a service*, following Christ the servant of all men.

The Church's tradition interprets this basic triple ministry according to the sociological situations of the time; it becomes diversified, multiplied and adapted; but it always reappears, as if in filigree, through the various ecclesiastical constitutions.

This local bishop, in the midst of the presbyterate, should not be seen as a bishop in the modern sense, the head of a large diocese and many priests; nor should he be compared to a Protestant pastor, surrounded by a lay presbyteral college, as in the Reformed Churches. The bishop in the presbyterate of the letters of St Ignatius is rather the pastor of a local urban church, surrounded by presbyters forming a college, and by deacons. Both are, properly speaking, ministers of Christ, in the service of God's people assembled in a community in the local church.

Thus, at the beginning of the second century, we see how the apostolic ministry, born out of Christ's will and institution, arrives at the triple ministry — episcopal, presbyteral and diaconal. This succession to the apostolic ministry, in the second half of the first century, seems organic and unbroken; it seems not to have raised any serious problems. The letters of St Ignatius of Antioch seem to be a homogeneous development of the Pastoral Epistles to Timothy and Titus, on the question of the organization of ministries in the Church. The bishop is the steward of God's house; his episcopate is not a monarchical power but a service linked to a presbyterate. The presbyters, grouped in a college, are the bishop's fellow workers, like the apostles around Christ. The deacons are the bishop's assistants, his fellow servants. It is indeed the essence of the apostolic ministry which is thus followed in the triple ministry, at the beginning of the second century, within the Churches of Asia Minor to whom Ignatius is writing. And it is thus, in its various forms, that the succession to the apostolic ministry is continued in the history of the Church.

7

PRIESTHOOD AND MINISTRY, GIFTS OF THE SPIRIT

To understand the originality of the priesthood of Christ and its relation with the priesthood of the whole Church and ministry in the Church, it is important to clarify the theological vocabulary of the subject. The New Testament uses the title of 'priest, *hiereus*' to indicate the man consecrated to a sacrificial priesthood in four precise and well-defined cases:

(a) of the Jewish priests (e.g. Acts 4.1)
(b) of the Gentile priests (Acts 14.13: priests of Zeus)
(c) of Christ (Epistle to the Hebrews)
(d) of all Christians (*hierateuma*: 1 Pet. 2.9; *hiereis*: Rev. 1.6; 5.10; 20.6)

Christ appears in the Epistle to the Hebrews as the perfect and definitive priest.[25] He is the fulfilment of the priesthood of Israel, after the unexpected order of Melchizedek, and after him there can no longer be any priests or sacrifices in the sense of the old covenant. His unique and perfect sacrificial priesthood which was internal and personal, fulfilled in the total offering of himself on the cross and in perpetual intercession before the Father, put an end to the existence of priests and sacrifices according to Jewish tradition, but was to be extended in his Body, the Church, in the form of the royal and prophetic priesthood of all Christians. So there are no priests, *hiereis*, except Christ and all the baptised.

In the New Testament the word priest, *hiereus*, is never applied to ministers of the Church.[26] Not even the Jewish priests converted to the Gospel (Acts 6.7) seem to have had any particular priestly position in the Church. Ministry in the

76

Church was exercised by apostles, prophets, evangelists, pastors, teachers, bishops, elders, deacons... (Eph. 4.11; Timothy and Titus), never by priests, by *hiereis*, by men consecrated to a sacrificial priesthood in the sense of the order of Aaron. Ministry in the Church is of a wholly original, new nature in relation to the sacrificial priesthood of the old covenant.

Christ's priesthood and that of the whole Church is an offering of sacrifice and intercession. Just as Christ offered himself as a sacrifice for the whole world, so each Christian offers his whole being as a living, holy and acceptable sacrifice, and with himself offers up the world to consecrate it to God in the Spirit and in truth. As Christ intercedes with the Father for all men, every Christian intercedes for all men that they may find salvation and happiness in Jesus Christ. So Christ's priesthood and that of the whole Church has as its essential function the consecration of the world to God in sacrifice and intercession. All Christians are priests, in the communion of Christ the priest, for the world and in the world.

Christ's ministry and that of the Church is to build and sanctify the community. As Christ proclaimed the good news of God's kingdom, performed signs of the presence and work of the Father, exercised the Holy Spirit's authority to create love and unity among the disciples, so ministry in the Church, which is the ministry of Christ through his ordained ministers, preaches the Gospel, administers the sacraments and exercises authority in the service of love and unity: '[Christ's] gifts were that some should be apostles, some prophets, some evangelists, some pastors and teachers, to equip the saints for the work of ministry (*diakonia*), for building up the body of Christ...' (Eph. 4.11–12). This ministry concerns the Church and all Christians, it is a ministry *ad intra*, it consitututes the building of the Body of Christ, the Church, through its head, Christ in glory (Eph. 4.13). Certain Christians are ministers, in the communion of Christ the deacon, pastor and bishop (John 13.14; Luke 22.26–27; John 10.11;1 Pet. 2.25; 5.1–4); they are chosen, called and ordained by Christ and given by him to the Church, to form the Body of Christ, to build up and sanctify God's people by the word, the sacraments and the spirit of power, love and self-control (2 Tim. 1.7).

The royal, prophetic priesthood of the whole people of God for the world and the ordained ministry in the Church to build up the Body of Christ both have as their aim God's praise and glory. The universal priesthood offers the world to consecrate it to God in sacrifice and intercession. The ordained ministry builds up the Body of Christ so that it may continue to grow as this royal, prophetic priesthood. The universal priesthood and the ordained ministry, whose aim is God's praise and glory, find their deepest unity in the worship offered to God and most particularly in the Eucharist, which brings about the communion of Christ's priesthood and ministry with the priesthood and ministry of the Church. Indeed, in the Eucharist, the gift of Christ's real presence, every Christian offers himself as a living, holy and acceptable sacrifice and intercedes for all men, at the foot of the cross and at one with the heavenly Intercessor; equally, in the Eucharist, the ministry of the Church is carried out in the preaching of God's word, in the celebration of the sacrament of Christ, and in assembling the Christian community in one body in love and unity, under the authority of the pastor and bishop of our lives, which is symbolized in the presidency of the ministers of the Church.

The universal priesthood of God's people and the ordained ministry in the Church exist, live and act in as much as they are sharing Christ's priesthood and ministry in communion with him.

By their participation in and fellowship with Christ the prophet, priest and king, Christians are signs and instruments of the Lord's priesthood in the world; they form a chosen race, a royal priesthood, a holy nation, God's own people, to proclaim the praises of him who has called us to offer spiritual sacrifices, acceptable to God through Jesus Christ and to maintain good conduct among the nations, so that through good deeds they may glorify God on the day of his visitation (1 Pet. 2.9,5,12). So Christ uses his Body, the Church, as a sign and instrument, to proclaim the Gospel in the world, to offer sacrifices to the Father according to the Spirit and to draw men, through the holiness of Christian life, to glorify God.

Through their participation and fellowship with Christ the deacon, pastor and bishop, ministers are the signs and instruments of the Lord's ministry in the Church; they constitute a council of ministers (1 Tim. 4.14), chosen, called and ordained by God to be given to the Church and to serve it, to organize and stimulate the royal and prophetic priesthood of the faithful, and to build up the community of the Body of Christ.

The ordained minister in the Church is firstly a servant of God's word. He has the spiritual gift of preaching the Gospel, the good news of salvation: in liturgical preaching, in teaching the catechism and in theological exposition. Secondly he officiates at Christ's sacraments: he presides over the celebration of the signs of the Lord's presence and action, for the sanctification of Christians. Thirdly, he represents the authority of the Holy Spirit: as the leader of a community, as a spiritual guide, having some of his Christian brethren in his care, he displays through his office the authority of the Spirit over human beings to make them grow in love and to keep unity among them.

The fact that ministry is not a sacrificial priesthood, in the sense of the old covenant, does not mean that it is a simple theological specialization within God's people. Ministry is the fruit of a calling from God, of preparation and ordination. The right to exercise a ministry in the Church cannot be assumed by just anyone. At times it has been argued that the Churches born of the Reformation rejected the traditional doctrine of the ordained ministry, because they did not teach the doctrine of a sacrifical priesthood. This erroneous idea may be dispelled if we take some texts from the Reformed tradition, which are useful, moreover, in clarifying certain aspects of ministry.

In reply to the question: 'Is it necessary... that pastors should preside over churches?' Calvin's Catechism replies: 'It is necessary to hear them and listen with fear and reverence to the doctrine of Christ as propounded from their lips... [Christ] has committed to the ministers of the Church the office of teaching in his name and stead'.[27] This clear affirmation of the need for ministry, in the chapter on God's word, is continued in the chapter on the sacraments. To the question 'Does the administration both of baptism and of the Supper belong indiscriminately to all?' the Catechism replies: 'It is confined to those to whom the office of teaching has been committed. For the two things, viz., to feed the Church with the doctrine of piety and administer the sacrament, are united together by an indissoluble tie'. Then to the question 'Can you prove this to me by the testimony of Scripture?' we find the reply: 'Christ gave special commandment to the apostles to baptize. In the celebration of the Supper he ordered us to follow his example. And the evangelists relate that he himself in dispensing it, performed the office of a public minister'.[28]

The doctrine that emerges from Calvin's Catechism is very precise. The pastor represents Christ, teaches the Lord's doctrine, celebrates the Holy Eucharist following Christ's example, when he ministered to the apostles on the evening of Maundy Thursday, baptizes and preaches in the succession of the apostles who received this commission from God; to distrust or pay no heed to the pastor is to reject Christ and be separated from the Church, because he is the representative of both.

The doctrine is again made clear in the Confessions of Faith. The Confession of La Rochelle (1559: articles XXIX–XXXII) and the Confession of the Netherlands (1571: articles XXX–XXXII) affirm that the true Church must be ruled according to the order established by Christ and taught according to his word.[29] They distinguish three ministries: the pastorate, the presbyterate and the diaconate; so there are in the Church pastors or ministers who preach and administer the sacraments, elders or overseers, who watch over the doctrine and the disciples of the community, and deacons who serve the poor and oppressed. The elders and deacons are 'like the senate of the Church'. All pastors have the 'same authority and equal power, under a single head, the one sovereign and one universal bishop, Jesus Christ'. These precepts are somewhat reminiscent of the ecclesiology of St Ignatius of Antioch, with his threefold ministry of the episcopate, presbyters and deacons, the presbytery representing the 'apostles' senate', and his idea of the invisible episcopacy of Christ over the Church. As a result it could legitimately be said that far from suppressing the episcopacy, the Reformed Churches multiplied it and established a bishop in each parish called a church, surrounded by a presbytery of elders and deacons. However, the situation evolved in the direction of laicizing the presbytery of the elders and the disappearance of deacons in many Churches. The Reformed Churches have thus been left with the single ministry of the pastor-overseer, assisted, in tasks which are too often solely material, by laymen who form a parish council. The Confessions of Faith insist on the necessity of being chosen by the Church to exercise these ministries: 'We believe that no one should interfere, on his own authority, in the government of the Church, but that this should be done by election... We believe that the ministers of God's word, elders and deacons, should be elected to their offices by a valid election by the Church, invoking God's name in good order, as God's word teaches. So let each man refrain from interfering by illegal means, but wait until such time as he is called by God, so that he may have evidence of his calling, to be assured and certain that it comes from God' (La Rochelle XXXI, Netherlands XXXI).[30] So the Reformation sees as legitimate a ministry constituted by vocation, election and invocation or ordination.

In the seventeenth century it is still the same doctrine of valid ministry that is being expressed among the Reformed. Jean Daillé, explaining the Catechism, writes firmly and unequivocally:

'Since the sacraments are part of the means of our salvation... it is clear that their administration belongs to the Pastors established in the Church to be Christ's ministers and to distribute his mysteries... That is why they are called "God's fellow workers" (1 Cor. 3.6–9)... The treasure of salvation has been entrusted to them, they have it, although earthly vessels... (If others are to administer them), that is taking away (from the Ministers) the honour of their duty and destroying God's institution and throwing his house into confusion... Only true and valid officers are fit to administer them, and if anyone undertakes to do so without receiving from Him that ministry and commission, he clearly becomes guilty of sacrilege and what he does is worthless'.[31] Pastor Chamier for his part says: 'The usual valid minister of the sacraments is not just anyone, not even a single Christian: but among Christians it can only be one who has been legitimately called to the ministry and who has been publicly charged with it... No reasonable person would hold all Christians equal in the administration of the word and sacraments: not only because everything in the Church must be done decently and in order, but also because, following Christ's own command, ministers are ordained for that'.[32]

If the Reformation strongly underlined the distinction between sacrificial priesthood, according to the old covenant, and evangelical ministry, it maintained the doctrine of the divine institution of ministries, their necessity for the Church, and ordination by the laying on of hands, the effective sign of the Holy Spirit.

Ministers and laity constitute one people, a single royal and prophetic priesthood, one undivided Church. Their unity is not helped if their separate vocations and service are confused. On the other hand it is helped and underlined if their respective functions in the people of God are well defined.

The ordained minister is primarily one of the faithful, a member of the universal priesthood. His ordination, which lays on him a ministry in the Church, does not take him out of the common condition of the laity. He is deeply at one with the life of the laity, closely united to all his fellow Christians in every aspect of his existence. These considerations must raise the question of the human and social life of ministers who participate fully in the common existence of all mankind, being distinguished from the laity only by vocation and ordination. Nowadays, for example, ought a minister of the Church to have a trade or profession like all other men? Has there not been too much insistance, particularly since the sixteenth century, on the university education of ministers? Does this education not risk making them into intellectuals, cut off from other Christians? To bring laymen into the universal priesthood and into Christian service, ought not the minister to be plunged into the same way of life?

According to the New Testament, presbyters are chosen because of their experience of life in the Church and their ability to teach God's word; they are not a theological aristocracy, but humble servants of the universal priesthood of all God's people. We must rediscover a presbyterate which is open more widely to everyone, less reserved for an intellectual élite. God's vocation to the ministry must not necessarily be channelled through universities and degrees. In this way the Church is depriving itself of a pastorate which would be in closer contact with layman of all sorts. If the Church wants to regain this contact with different social categories it does not just need intellectual pastors, but also working-class pastors... pastors whose education has not gradually cut them off from their original background. The Church today needs ministers who are less clerical and less intellectual. This does not rule out a good biblical and theological training for ministers, but this training could be shorter and more basic than university studies, which are often wide-ranging. More advanced and more technical theological training for some who are suited to it and good as it could lead them to a ministry of theological teaching. Thus we should regain the ministry of the teacher, who would not just be a university professor, but a pastor theologian at the service of his colleagues in the ministry.

Mission and ministry in the Church are the work of the Holy Spirit sent by the Father and the Son. The Church's mission and ministry can only exist in the power of the Holy Spirit, sent from the Father and in the name of Christ. The Holy Spirit makes God's word fully effective, fulfilling the promise contained in the sacraments and uniting the Christian community by spreading love among it. So the whole mission and ministry of the Church supposes a constant epiclesis of the Spirit, a prayer that the Holy Spirit may open Men's hearts to God's word, that it may work to make the sacraments effective signs of Christ's presence, and that Christians may be united in one living body in the same brotherly love. The whole life of the Son of God in his incarnation in word and deed was accomplished in the power of the Holy Spirit. It was the Holy Spirit that conceived Christ in Mary on the day of the incarnation, gave him the messianic anointing at his baptism in the Jordon, and filled him with the power for his ministry (see Luke 1.35; 3.22; 4.1,14,18–19 etc.). The Holy Spirit's role at the time of the incarnation was to show Christ's constant dependence on his Father: he did nothing that the Father did not tell him to do, he did it in the power of the Spirit. The mention of the work of the Spirit in the life of Christ underlines the fact that the Son's incarnation did not exhaust the Father's work, that it remained an action willed by the Father and sustained by the Holy Spirit. The Spirit's role in the earthly life of the Son underlines the trinitarian action at the incarnation and rules out any christomonism in theological thought. Christ was only the fullness of God because he was the Son sent by the Father and because he lived, spoke and acted in the power of the Spirit.

At Pentecost the apostles received the fullness of the Holy Spirit in accordance with Christ's promise; the Spirit would be for them the other Paraclete to be with them always, the Spirit of truth who would guide them into all truth (John 14.16; 16.13). The Spirit would not exhaust God's action after Pentecost any more than the Son had, by himself, been the fullness of God in his incarnation: the Spirit would not speak on his own authority, he would speak whatever he heard, he would glorify Christ, he would take what belonged to the Son and declare it to the apostles, he would teach them all things and bring to their remembrance all that Christ had told them (John 16.13–14; 14.26). The Father would send the Holy Spirit in the Son's name; all that the Father had belonged to the Son, which was why the Spirit would take from the Son what he would give to the apostles and to the Church (John 14.26; 16.15). The Holy Spirit would therefore show himself to the apostles as a person, the other Paraclete who would be at their side and whom they could invoke as their councellor, their consolation and their defence. He stayed with them and was even in them (John 14.17). It was the Holy Spirit, sent by the Father, as witness to the Son, who clothed the apostles in power in the exercise of their mission and ministry. It was the Spirit whom they transmitted to men through God's word, through baptism and the laying on of hands. The Holy Spirit is a person, a power and a gift of God, whom the apostles could pass on, having received him in fullness.

Since Pentecost the Holy Spirit has bestowed his gifts on the Church. It is the Spirit who creates faith in the hearts of Christians, who brings them to Christ and his Body to baptism, who makes clear to them the word of God, arouses their love and consolidates their unity in the Church, who gives them power to be Christ's witnesses in the world. It is the Holy Spirit who gives to some gifts for ministry (1 Cor.12.4–11). The Holy Spirit distributes his gifts as he sees fit, a great variety of gifts corresponding to the variety of ministries. It is the task of the Church to recognize these gifts and make use of them, for the manifestation of the Spirit is given for the common good (1 Cor. 12.7). It is in this way that the Church recognized that God had given it and established in it firstly apostles, secondly prophets, thirdly teachers, then gifts of power, then spiritual gifts of healing, helpers, administrators and speakers in various tongues (1 Cor. 12.27–28; Eph. 4.11–12). From the Holy Spirit there originates the variety both of gifts and of the organization of ministries for building the Body of Christ; it is always the same Spirit who is at work in every gift and every ministry (1 Cor. 12.4–6) to build up the Body of Christ. There is no possible contradiction between a charismatic or pneumatic conception of the Church and a ministerial or institutional one. The two most important Pauline writings or ministries in the Church are quite explicit: the Holy Spirit allocates gifts and ministries, he organizes gifts into ministries (Eph. 4.11–12), he appoints the charismatic ministries (1 Cor. 12.28). There is one Body and Spirit (Eph. 4.4); there can be no contradiction between the distribution of gifts according to the Spirit's will and the organization of ministries in the Body of Christ. A ministry in the Body of Christ presupposes a gift of the Holy Spirit; a gift of the Spirit is bestowed in order to establish a ministry in the Body of Christ. If, theologically, there is no contradiction between the Body and the Spirit, between ministries and gifts, if both are intended for each other for the common good and growth of the Church, it may nonetheless be noted that the balance has not always been maintained in the practise of the Church. One Church, more conscious of the organization of the Body and the order of the ministries, will overlook the need for gifts, fear the freedom of the Spirit, be closed to prophetic renewal and halt the spread of a variety of ministries. Another Church, more alert to the life of the Spirit and the distribution of gifts, will overlook the need for ministries, fear the institution of the Church, distrust traditional continuity and prevent gifts being organized into ordered ministries. It is clear that for St Paul neither is right; both are wrong precisely because they distrust the elements they fear. It is the balance between a just recognition of spiritual gifts, the freedom of the Spirit, the spirit of prophecy and the variety of ministries, and a sound conception of the ministry, institution, continuity and ordination, that the ecumenical truth of ecclesiology is to be found.

Since the overriding tendency for the Church, as for society, is to become over-institutionalized in organizing its ministries and so to lose the charismatic and prophetic spirit, God maintains alongside the Church Christian communities which reject ministerial institutions in favour of spiritual freedom, so that through them the Church may be constantly aware of the work of the Holy Spirit who distributes gifts most fittingly and makes heard the prophetic call where he wills, for the good of the Body of Christ. Would that the Church might always recognize the providential role of these communities and not judge them according to the criteria of its theology or its law, but according to the fruits of the Spirit which they produce!

PART THREE

EPISCOPATE, PRESBYTERATE AND DIACONATE

8

THE EPISCOPATE

Without prejudging the variety of ministries, which can multiply according to the gifts of the Spirit and the needs of the Church, it must be recognized that the three ministries, episcopal, presbyteral and deaconal, always reappear in tradition in various forms due to historical and sociological circumstances.

In the forms of the early second century the *episkopos* is identified with the local or parish pastor and is surrounded by a presbytery and deacons who are his assistants. In later or modern forms of Catholicism the bishop has at times an immense area in which to exercise his ministry and he is more replaced, than assisted, by numerous presbyters in charge of the parishes of his diocese. His task of co-ordination and organization takes a big place alongside his pastoral ministry; often he becomes an administrator as much as a pastor. The doctrine of the Second Vatican Council seeks to restore the whole pastoral dimension of the episcopate.

The Church's present situation demands a broader episcopate than the Reformed pastorate, and one which is more pastoral than the Catholic episcopacy of recent centuries. In this situation the local or parish presbyterate assumes a greater importance and autonomy: the local pastor takes on certain characteristics of the second-century over-seer. Several functions of the episcopal ministry are similar to those of the elders; they are exercised by the bishop, in fellowship with them, to serve all the church communities in his charge. We could therefore begin by examining the presbyteral ministry; but it is preferable to look first at the episcopal ministry which has a unifying function in the local church, allowing us to leave to the next chapter certain basic aspects of the ministry which are equally relevant to the episcopate and the presbyterate, since it is true that the overseer is a pastor among pastors, an overseer in the presbytery, following the idea of St Ignatius of Antioch. So it must always be borne in mind that the particular ministry of the bishop is added to the pastoral ministry which he has already known and exercised as a presbyter. There is no question here of treating all aspects of the episcopal ministry. Many excellent studies appeared in the 1950s and 60s on the subject, particularly in preparation for the Second Vatican Council and the various plans for uniting the Churches belonging to the World Council of Churches at Geneva.[1] We should like just to indicate a few points concerning the renewal of the episcopal ministry of the Churches today.

The bishop is the visible head of the regional church or of a particular mission of the Church. He is the visible sign of the invisible episcopacy of Christ in the Church. He carries out this episcopal function in the fellowship of the presbytery, that is pastors who minister in the region or in the mission entrusted to him, and in fellowship with other bishops, with whom he shares the episcopacy of the universal Church. He is also actively in contact with deacons and laymen whom he draws into his work in the Church. His ministry, like that of the pastors, is a ministry of the word, sacraments and authority of the Spirit in the service of charity and unity in the Church.

The bishop is essentially God's steward (*oikonomos*, Titus 1.7). As he rules his own house, so he must rule God's house which is the Church. 'For if a man does not know how to manage his own household, how can he care for God's church?' (1 Tim. 3.5). The apostles were the first apostles of the Church, followed by their helpers and immediate successors like Timothy and Titus, who were charged with keeping the faith, ordaining ministers and managing God's house. As the stewards of God's house, the bishops are the apostles' successors, in that part of their ministry that could be handed down.

The Pastor and the Evangelist

In the early Church we can see two different episcopal functions which have a place in the apostolic succession. First there is the assimilation of the apostle's successor to *the overseer in the presbytery* of a local community. For St Ignatius the very college of presbyters represents the 'apostles' senate' around Christ, whose invisible episcopacy was symbolized by the overseer. But, in general, it was the local overseer who assumed the function of stewardship in God's house, exercised first by the apostles, then by their helpers and immediate successors. Stewardship and apostolic government was geographically fixed in the ministry of the local overseer surrounded by the presbytery and deacons. In confusing the apostle's successor with the overseer in the presbytery of the local community, there was the risk of losing the availability of the apostles and their successors for mission and for founding Churches. But there existed precisely in the ancient Church a missionary ministry, that of the *evangelist*, also considered as an apostolic successor. We find this word evangelist three times in the New Testament: it is used of Philip, one of the seven ordained by the apostles at Jerusalem (Acts 6.5–6; 21.8), and Timothy, God's fellow-worker in the Gospel of Christ (1 Thess. 3.2; 2 Tim. 4.5); it figures in Paul's list of ministries: 'apostles, prophets, evangelists, pastors and teachers' (Eph. 4.11). The evangelist's duty is to proclaim the Gospel, hence his name (Acts 8.4–5,12,35,40; 1 Thess. 3.2; Phil. 2.22); he is subordinate to the apostles (Acts 8. 14 ff; Eph. 4.11). Thus, in the ancient Church, evangelists were considered successors to the apostles, itinerants and missionaries. Eusebius describes the ministry of the evangelists as follows: 'Many others were well known at this time, belonging to the first stage in the apostolic succession. These earnest disciples of great men built on the foundations of the churches everywhere laid by the apostles, spreading the message still further and sowing the saving seed of the Kingdom of Heaven far and wide through the entire world. Very many of the disciples of the time, their hearts smitten by the word of God with an ardent passion for true philosophy, first fulfilled the Saviour's command by distributing their possessions among the needy; then, leaving their homes behind, they carried out the work of evangelists, ambitious to preach to those who had never heard the message of the faith and to give them the inspired gospels in writing. Staying only to lay the foundations of the faith in one foreign place or another, appoint others as pastors, and entrust to them the tending of those newly brought in, they set off again for other lands and peoples with the grace and cooperation of God... It is impossible for me to enumerate by name all who in the first succession from the apostles became pastors or evangelists in the churches of the known world'.[2] Then Eusebius names Ignatius of Antioch and Clement of Alexandria because they were known through their letters. So Eusebius appears to be describing on the one hand a succession of the apostles in a ministry of building up the Churches: according to the form described by St Ignatius of Antioch it is a question of *pastors-overseers* and a succession of the apostles in a ministry of evangelism and of foundation: that of the *missionary-evangelists* according to the example of Philip in the Acts of the Apostles (Acts 6.5–6; 8.4 ff,12,35,40). So there is a double apostolic succession: that of the pastors-overseers who build up and rule over Churches already established, and that of missionary-evangelists who preach the Gospel and found new Churches.

One might wonder whether the circumstances of modern life, the demands of evangelism and the needs of a Christianized and dechristianized world, do not militate today in favour of adopting the distinction between two basic forms of the episcopate in the apostolic succession: a pastoral episcopate and an evangelistic episcopate. The first would correspond more to the episcopate in the presbytery of St. James at Jerusalem or according to St Ignatius of Antioch, while the second would be more in the line of the itinerant episcopacy of the evangelists, missionaries and founders, like Philip and Timothy, following the example of the apostles.

The resident bishop was charged particularly with the stewardship of God's house, in its localized form of a regional church. He was entrusted to keep the faith, he organized and ordered the various ministries, he headed church government, and maintained the external relations between the local church and the other churches and the world. He was pastor of the various ministers of his Church. His ministry of government was not exercised on his own personal authority, but in the name of Christ, the invisible Shepherd and

Guardian of souls (1 Pet. 2.25). So it was by God's word that he ruled God's Church. He was the ambassador and sign of Christ, the chief Shepherd (1 Pet. 5.4). That is why he had to be capable of the evangelistic and apostolic teaching of which he was the trustee and guardian (Titus 1.9; 1 Tim. 6.20). On the other hand he did exercise his ministry of government *in presbyterio*, in the fellowship of the college of presbyters, in the community of the other ministers of the local church and also in fellowship with other bishops of the universal Church, regrouped in national conferences. The Church's constitution had to allow for this situation of episcopal government in the presbyteral college, the limits and control of this episcopal government by the collegiality of presbyters and of bishops; it was a system of episcopal-presbyteral-collegiate government, after the idea of St Ignatius.

The evangelist bishop had to have as his primary task mission to non-Christians, the evangelizing of post-Christians and the renewal of the Church. Following the example of the apostles and evangelists he had to be itinerant and ready to serve all the Churches. His function was to stimulate the foundation of new Christian communities, to suit the different settings and conditions of contemporary life, to organize and order the first ministries in the unexplored areas of the world, to foster new forms of prayer and to suggest new ways of preaching; it was also his duty to promulgate renewal in all areas of the Christians life, establishing ecumenical links between the Churches. His ministry would mean witnessing new situations of modern life and engaging in dialogue, to instruct the leaders of Churches on current major problems. He could be attached both to a local church and to an ecumenical, international body of Churches. His function was to set out the primordial missionary character of the Church and the need for its ecumenical unity. The Anglican Bishop John Robinson has written that today the Church is faced with the need both to reform its existing structures and to discover new ones beginning with the world's problems: he calls this 'starting from the other end'.[3] That is something profoundly true. As far as the episcopal ministry is concerned it means that the Church must both renew the ministry of the pastor-overseer with historic tradition as its starting point, and rediscover the ministry of the bishop-evangelist starting from the problems posed by today's world.

The two forms of episcopacy that we have distinguished both include *doctrinal, liturgical* and *ecumenical* functions. With the elders, whose pastor he is, the bishop shares the duty and service of the word, the sacraments and unity. However, as steward of God's house, as a visible head of the Church, the bishop has a doctrinal, liturgical and ecumenical ministry that is his alone.

Teacher of the Church and Pastor of the Pastors

The bishop is a teacher of the Church. He is responsible for proclaiming the Gospel of Christ, for doctrine, preaching and the catechism. He is the first to be charged to guard the truth entrusted to him by the Holy Spirit who dwells in him (2 Tim. 1.14; 1 Tim. 6.20). As God's steward he must 'hold firm to the sure word as taught, so that he may be able to give instruction in sound doctrine and also to confute those who contradict it' (Titus 1.9). He is the promulgator and guardian of the sound doctrine of Christ. As such, he runs the risk of timidity and fear, if he cares excessively for the integrity of the faith; he must remember that he did not receive a spirit of timidity, but the Holy Spirit which is power, love and wisdom (2 Tim. 1.7). The power of the Spirit and the love of all men give him the courage and audacity to adapt the Gospel message to contemporary questions raised by the modern world; the wisdom of the Spirit and self-control lead him to guard faithfully the fundamental truths of the faith, without which preaching would be just another example of human wisdom. It is in this tension between the need to stimulate the development of faith and the responsibility of guarding the faith entrusted to him that the doctrinal ministry of the bishop lies. It may well happen that he has to 'confute those who contradict' in order to safeguard the 'sound doctrine', but it will always be with love and self-control, with the sole concern of maintaining the faith, not to defend personal opinions, whether conservative or progressive. The bishop's doctrinal authority is a difficult responsibility which demands of him a deep love for God's world, considerable theological knowledge and thorough understanding of man and the world. He exercises this doctrinal ministry with his pastors to stimulate their preaching, and with the laity to renew the sense of their presence and witness in the world.

Thus, by means of God's word, he builds up the ordained ministry in the Church and the priesthood of all the faithful. This doctrinal ministry is also collegiate. The bishop does not carry it out alone but in fellowship with the whole presbytery which is entrusted to him, and also in fellowship with the other bishops whom he meets in episcopal conferences. The ecumenical council is the supreme form of this doctrinal ministry of the bishops, who assemble in the service of the universal Church. In this ministry the bishop takes counsel from the laity of his Church; he is alert to their needs and opinions, for it is only in this way that he can be assured that his thinking corresponds to the current will of God and that his teaching is effective in regard to modern man. Besides, his doctrinal ministry is concerned solely with teaching the Gospel in the realm of Christian faith, prayer and Christian life; as far as the particular responsibilities of the laity in their priesthood are concerned with respect to the world and in their life among men, the bishop will take care to leave them free to make their own choices and decisions in obedience to faith and charity.

Since he has the pastoral care of his Church and is responsible for preaching the Gospel, it is natural that the bishop should be concerned with new vocations, ensuring the preparation of future pastors and introducing them into ministry through ordination. The laying on of hands which ordains a minister is an apostolic and collegiate act. Timothy was instructed to remember his ordination by the laying on of hands by Paul (2 Tim. 1.6) and by the council of the elders (1 Tim. 4.14). It was with the presbytery that the bishop ordained ministers.[4] In this way the fact is revealed that the new pastor is incorporated into the ministerial body, which serves the priestly body of all God's people. The presbytery acts there as a sign of the college of the apostles, who were the first to establish ministries in the Church. Catholic tradition, in its ordination rite, has always associated the presbytery with the bishop in the central act of the laying on of hands, forming a collegiate episcopacy. Basically, the Reformed tradition of the sixteenth century has shown in practice that the apostolic succession of the ministry was being fulfilled through the collegiate ordination of pastors, representing, as St Ignatius said, the 'apostles' senate'. The historical and ecumenical evolution of the Reformed tradition tends today to make it recognize the good foundation of a form of regional episcopacy, distinct from the parish pastorate. Since 1918 German Lutheranism has seen, in a fairly general way, the re-establishing of regional episcopacy, with Lutheran bishops replacing the princes or civil authorities in the responsibilities of Church government. The Scandinavian Lutherans have never lost a regional episcopacy, since there the church structure has been completely maintained. These differences show that Reformed or Lutheran Protestantism is not opposed to the episcopal structure of the Church, provided that the collegiate nature of this episcopacy is maintained, in the presbytery and in fellowship with other bishops. The ecumenical call to unity urges the Churches to seek again a sense of the episcopal ministry which conforms to Scripture and to ancient tradition, adapting to the circumstances of the modern world and to bringing about the visible unity of the divided Churches. So the bishop and the presbytery, representing the college of the apostles in the ordination rite, symbolize the mission which God gives today as always to new pastors and the apostolic succession of the ministry in the Church. They ordain these new ministers by laying hands on them and invoking the gifts of the Holy Spirit, thus incorporating them into the ministerial body to build up and sanctify the royal and prophetic priesthood of all the people of God. We shall see later the significance of ordination and the problems involved. The bishop also takes part, with others, in the consecration of new bishops. Thus every ordination or consecration in the Church has a collegiate nature, recalling the collegiality of the apostles, and thereby symbolizing the apostolic succession of the ministry and the mission given by God himself to his ministers in the power of the Holy Spirit.

Some Churches entrust the bishop with the liturgical act of confirmation. This function is not necessarily his alone. However, the reason is understandable. If confirmation is seen as the consecration of the laity to service in the Church, it may be significant that the bishop, who is responsible for preaching the Gospel, and for ministry and service in the Church, should perform the rite of confirming-consecrating the baptised. It could be the time to celebrate confirmations at a regional level and thus to give a wider aspect to this commissioning of laymen in the regional church. However, confirmation in the setting of the local community is at times preferable and, in this case, it is right that it should be performed by the presbyters, the pastors of the local community.

When the bishop celebrates the Eucharist, it is significant that he is surrounded by presbyters and deacons who take part in the celebration. Thus, in the course of an act which is essential to the life of the Church, there is clearly visible the sign of the ministry united round the bishop and of the collegiate nature of his presidency in the midst of the presbytery. When St Ignatius of Antioch spoke of the over-seer 'with the fitly wreathed spiritual circlet of your presbytery, and with the deacons who walk after God' (Magn. XIII) he must have had in mind the celebration of the Eucharist by the bishop surrounded by presbyters and deacons. This concelebration is a sign of a united ministry and of the unity of the Church. Elsewhere he says again: 'Be ye careful therefore to observe one eucharist (for there is one flesh of our Lord Jesus Christ and one cup into union in his blood; there is one altar, as there is one bishop, together with the presbytery and the deacons my fellow-servants)' (Phil. IV). This vision of the overseer with the presbytery and deacons, concelebrating the Eucharist at the same altar, is the finest symbol of the episcopal ministry in collegiality, to serve the ministers of the Church and all the people of God in unity.

Ecumenical Servant

The bishop is the pastor of the regional church. He is responsible for its internal unity and its communion with other Churches. That is his particular ecumenical function. He must take care of God's Church and manage it as his own house (1 Tim. 3.4–5). His authority within the presbytery is for charity and unity within the Church. He is at once the sign of Christ, ruling his Church unseen, and the sign of the Spirit, stimulating charity and bringing about unity in the Christian community.

His pastoral-episcopal authority, the sign of the authority of Christ the invisible shepherd-guardian of our lives (1 Pet. 2.25) is exercised in the Church like that of the shepherd over his flock. Since the term shepherd is applied to ministry in the New Testament, we can recall here the parable of the good shepherd (John 10.11–16) and the mission given to Peter to tend Christ's sheep (John 21.15–17). Just as Christ is the good shepherd of the Church because he gave his life for the Church, and just as the pastoral ministry of Peter is founded on the love of Christ, so the bishop's ministry of authority for charity and unity proceeds from his love for Christ and lies essentially in the gift of his life for those entrusted to him. He knows that Christ the good shepherd became the lamb slaughtered for man's salvation. His authority is wholly gentleness, kindliness and patience. He does not exercise an authoritarian power which is imposed by force, but watchful service which is carried out in love. He knows that God's word alone has undeniable authority, so that it alone can persuade men to obey Christ and lead to unity of the Spirit. So it is essentially through God's word and as his servant that he can exercise valid authority and control in the Church. Like St Paul, the strength of his ministry is in his weakness; he knows that human weakness accepted in humility serves the glory of God better than personal power. The bishop would be going against his function of service under Christ's authority if, as St Peter writes, he was 'domineering over those in [his] charge'; quite on the contrary, like the good shepherd who gives his life for his sheep, he must be an example to his flock (1 Pet. 5.3). He is not a prince, but the humble servant of the Lord of the Church, awaiting the appearance of Christ the chief shepherd, from whom he will receive 'the unfading crown of glory' (1 Pet. 5.4). He will only share this glory on the last day if he is a true witness of the sufferings of Christ (1 Pet. 5.1).

The qualities of the bishop and his authority do not depend just on his obedience to Christ, the good shepherd, but also on the attitude of those who are in his charge. There is close solidarity between the shepherd and the flock, between the bishop and the Church he rules. As Christ said: 'I am the good shepherd, I know my own and my own know me' (John 10.14). And again: '[The shepherd of the sheep] goes before them and the sheep follow him, for they know his voice. A stranger they will not follow, but they will flee from him, for they do not know the voice of strangers' (John 10.4–5). The faithful and the ministers of the Church heed God's word proclaimed by the bishop, they recognize it and follow the bishop, or, rather, they obey the word of God which he preaches. The bishop, then, is renewed and encouraged in his ministry by the people of God who recognize in him the sign and word of the good shepherd and the unseen bishop of the Church: 'Obey your leaders and submit to them; for they are keeping watch over your souls, as men who will have to give account. Let them do this joyfully and not sadly, for that would be of no advantage to you... Remember your leaders, those who spoke to you the word of God; consider the outcome of their life and imitate their faith' (Heb. 13.17,7). The joy of ministry and the spiritual freedom of the bishop are reinforced by the objectivity of the mission he has received. We see at times in non-episcopal Churches that the necessary presidential authority is exercised almost guiltily, which leads to two impossible attitudes: slackness or authoritarianism. Often, authority without explicit theological or sacramental foundation callapses, or, conversely, is imposed in order to survive. By accepting a sound doctrine of the episcopate, presidential authority is freed from psychological inferiority or superiority complexes, and this allows a balanced government because it is accepted on both sides as a government of God's word through the bishop, the sign of Christ and instrument of the Spirit. The spiritual objectivity of episcopal authority, which allows it to be exercised freely and accepted readily, is basically safeguarded by three factors: a sound doctrine of the collegiality of bishops, the fair election of the bishop, and ordination by the laying on of hands invoking the gifts of the Spirit. These objective elements of his ministry will thus provide firm and liberating support for his authority and government. Obedience to the bishop will be even more spiritual and free, since it will quite consciously not be directed just to a man but to a minister called by God's word, because he is a sign of the invisible episcopacy of Christ, justly instituted in the Church and truly consecrated in the strength, love and wisdom of the Holy Spirit.

The bishop, as spiritual head of the regional church, shows in his person the unity of the Christian community in his charge. More than any other his word represents the common thought of God's people. St Ignatius of Antioch wrote to the Ephesians: 'In God's name I have received your whole multitude in the person of Onesimus, whose love passeth utterance and who is moreover your bishop in the flesh'

(Eph. I). The bishop represents and stimulates unity in the regional Church; equally he represents and stimulates the unity of the regional church with other regional churches, with the universal Church. Through the bishop the ministers are in fellowship with the universal ministry, and the local community is in fellowship with the Church in her catholicity.

The bishop's relationship with the world is also part of his ecumenical ministry. His ministry is not only that of the internal unity of the regional church or its unity with other churches, it is also the ministry of opening up the Church to the world and of the reconciliation of all mankind. He must be 'hospitable (*philoxenos:* friend of strangers), a lover of goodness, master of himself, upright, holy, and self-controlled... He must be well thought of by outsiders' (Titus 1.8; 1 Tim. 3.2,7). He has a ministry to receive all men. Being hospitable he loves those who say they are outside the Church. He recognizes good wherever it may be and he is the defender of justice among men. He does not fear dialogue with the secular authorities to defend the rights of good and of justice. So that this dialogue may be uncompromising and fraternal he remains entirely free with respect to civil authority, he is always master of himself and self-controlled. He knows that even for the world, even if he is not understood by the world, he is still a witness of holiness with respect to God. He performs a ministry of reconciliation among men, with the certainty of being a living link between the Church and the world. The fact that outsiders will think well of him will be for him a sign of the authenticity of his ecumenical ministry. He could not be a good bishop if outsiders were hostile to him, unless that hostility sprang from his honesty in defending good and justice, in his moderation and self-control.

The Collegiality of Brother Ministers

This ecumenical ministry of the bishop is based on presbyteral and episcopal collegiality. Because he rules the regional church in fellowship and in collaboration with the presbyters, he represents and brings about the unity of the universal Church which lies in the union of the regional churches among themselves. This presbyteral and episcopal collegiality is based on fraternity in the ministry. The bishop is the brother of the other bishops. Christ himself called the apostles 'brothers' when, risen from the dead, he said to Mary Magdalene: 'Go to my brethren and say to them, I am ascending to my Father and your Father, to my God and your God' (John 20.17). Before his passion Christ had already said to the apostles: 'No longer do I call you servants (*doulos* in the sense of slavery, not of service), for the servant does not know what his master is doing; but I have called you friends, for all that I have heard from my Father I have made known to you' (John 15.15). Because his apostles are sons of the Father, Christ calls them his brothers; because he shares with them knowledge of the Father he calls them his friends. If there is this relationship of fraternity and friendship between Christ and his apostles, it exists *a fortiori* between the overseer and his presbyters. The collegiality between the bishop, the sign of Christ the overseer, and the presbytery, the sign of the apostles' senate, is a brotherly and friendly collegiality. Christ charged Peter with strengthening his brethren (Luke 22.32). Thus the first apostle could not rule as master over the others, but his mission was to strengthen them in the faith, as his brothers. Christ had made it very clear to the apostles that they were all brothers and that the greatest among them was to be like a servant to the others (*diakonos*, Matt. 23.8,11). That is also true, *a fortiori*, for the overseer with respect to the other ministers in the Church. Thus, the bishop's authority has to be shown in fraternity and friendship within the presbytery and the church community. The bishop has to accept his authority as being in the service of others, whom he considers friends and brothers.

Christ's warnings to his apostles must be remembered here: 'But you are not to be called rabbi, for you have one teacher, and you are all brethren. And call no man your father on earth, for you have one Father, who is in heaven. Neither be called masters, for you have one master, the Christ. He who is greatest among you shall be your servant; whoever exalts himself will be humbled, and whoever humbles himself will be exalted' (Matt. 23.8–12). This passage does not rule out all order, since it talks of the greatest who must become a servant; but here Christ is warning against the temptation of titles and forms. The Scribes and Pharisees were accused by Christ of succumbing to that temptation: 'They do all their deeds to be seen by men' (Matt. 23.5–7). It cannot be thus for the apostles and their successors in the ministry of authority. By the invitation not to be called 'father' Christ draws attention to the unique fatherhood of God and the danger, in a ministry of authority, of a certain paternal possessiveness and paternalistic authoritarianism. Yet, if Christ warns against titles which could be tempting for authority, he does not forbid the paternal compassion which the apostle, or his successor, might feel for those whom he has brought into the faith and who are entrusted to his pastoral ministry. The bishop must not exercise a paternalistic authority which would obscure the unique fatherhood of God, but he may feel a father's concern for those who have been born to faith thanks to his ministry and whom he has guided in their spiritual lives as a true servant of the word of the one Father of the faithful. St Paul wrote to the Corinthians: 'Though you have countless guides in Christ you do not have many fathers. For I became your father in Christ Jesus through the Gospel' (1 Cor. 4.15). And to the Thessalonians: 'You know how, like a father with his children we exhorted each one of you and encouraged and charged you to lead a life worthy of God, who calls you into his own kingdom and glory' (1 Thess. 2.11–12). Spiritual fatherhood lies essentially in the fact of seriously exhorting the faithful, gently consoling them and gravely imploring them to lead them to God. The bishop, like the apostle, watches over the salvation of the souls for whom he will have to answer, as a father watches over his child.

The bishop has a particular ministry with other ministers of the Church. He is the pastor of pastors in the regional church. He is charged to nourish their faith, develop their spiritual lives, deepen their theological knowledge and guide their pastoral thinking. He is charged with strengthening his brothers in the ministry, like Peter among the apostles: 'I have prayed for you', Christ said to Peter, 'that your faith may not fail; and when you have turned again, strengthen your brethren' (Luke 22.32). Jesus foretold Peter's denial but promised him that, in spite of that, his faith would not fail and after his repentance he would increase the faith of his brothers, the rest of the apostles. The bishop shares this ministry of Peter's among the apostles: as leader in the presbytery his function is to strengthen his brother ministers, despite his own weakness and possible denials, for the Lord upholds his faith so that he may in his turn uphold that of others. His episcopal ordination has given him that mission and bestowed on him the gifts of the Spirit to carry it out.

The Patriarchy

The collegiate unity of bishops may demand church structures which foster and help it at national or universal level. If the bishop has a pastoral ministry to the presbyters in the regional church, if he is to them like Peter to the other apostles, is there a similar ministry to the overseers themselves? Is there a pastor to the bishops sharing for them in the ministry of Peter, strengthening their faith and their episcopal ministry, and working thus for the unity of the episcopate and of the universal Church? Calvin, describing the ministry in the ancient Church, spoke thus of the institutions of patriarchs: 'As to the fact that each province had an archbishop among the bishops... and, moreover, that in the Council of Nicea patriarchs were appointed to be superior to archbishops, in order and dignity, this was designed for the preservation of discipline, although, in treating of the subject here, it ought not to be omitted, that the practice was very rare. The chief reason for which these orders were instituted was, that if anything occurred in any church which could not well be explicated by a few, it might be referred to a provincial synod. If the magnitude or difficulty of the case demanded a larger discussion, patriarchs were employed along with synods, and from them there was no appeal except to a General Council. To the government thus constituted some gave the name of Hierarchy — a name, in my opinion, improper, certainly one not used by Scripture. For the Holy Spirit designed to provide that no one should dream of primacy or domination in regard to the government of the Church. But if, regarding the term, we look to the thing, we shall find that the ancient bishops had no wish to frame a form of church government different from that which God has prescribed in his word'.[5] It is interesting to note here that Calvin, while disliking the word hierarchy, sees the organization of the ancient Church at the time of the first four ecumenical Councils (fourth-fifth centuries) as conforming to God's word. The order of bishops, archbishops and patriarchs seems to him valid 'to preserve ecclesiastical order', that is to serve the unity of the universal Church. Admittedly Calvin thinks that this order was subsequently distorted, but he is offering here an ecumenical opening from which we should profit. In any case let it not be said that the episcopal and patriarchal structure is unacceptable to the Reformed Churches; that would be in contradiction to the thinking of the Reformer himself. What he wanted to maintain at all costs in the government of the Church was evangelical simplicity and the spirit of service, excluding all principality and domination contrary to Scripture.

Would it not be healthy for the Churches in the West to revert to a true patriarchal structure like the Churches of the East or of Eastern Europe? If the bishops are regrouped collegiately in episcopal conferences, it is right that their episcopal college should be presided over by a patriarch? He then is the bishops' pastor, sharing the ministry of Peter among the other apostles, strengthening his fellow bishops in faith and in their episcopal ministry. In the present ecumenical dialogue aimed at uniting separated Churches these problems of church government must be seen essentially in a pastoral sense and not, as often, from a point of view which is too exclusively theological or even legalistic. Before creating a theology of the episcopate or of the patriarchy, its deeply pastoral and fraternal function in the local and universal Church must be seen. The bishop must be seen firstly as the pastor of presbyters and deacons. The patriarch must be seen firstly as the pastor of the overseers. It is also good to consider the sharing of Peter's ministry, strengthening the faith of his fellow apostles, at different levels of the universal Church. This episcopal and patriarchal order is a pastoral service to strengthen faith, ministry and unity; it serves the unanimity of the universal Church in the plurality of local Churches.

The patriarch must have a role of overseer-primate in the conference of bishops; it is a pastoral function among the bishops, which at times may become a function of arbitration in times of difficulty or crisis. As Calvin said, this is good 'for keeping the ecclesiastical order', that is for maintaining and developing unity. In the ecumenical council, bringing together all the patriarchs and bishops of the universal Church, a patriarch-primate may have this role of pastor and arbitrator. Here we are touching on the problem of the historical role of the bishop of Rome. This problem falls outside the scope of this book. However, it must be noted here that when this problem arises in ecumenical dialogue it must not be seen primarily on the ecclesiological and judicial level, but primarily on the pastoral level: the possible role of a patriarch-primate with a function as pastor and arbitrator within the universal Church. Pope John XXIII gave us a good illustration of this pastoral and arbitrating ministry, in the Second Vatican Council and in the renewal of the Catholic Church. Pope Paul VI, continuing this task, wanted to give a new fraternal and ecumenical style to this ministry of the 'servant of God's servants'.

The rediscovery of the authentic episcopal ministry is essential today in seeking Christian unity. The Second Vatican Council made an enormous effort to explore in greater depth the doctrine of the episcopate. The meetings of certain Churches who belong to the World Council of Churches always raise this problem of the episcopate, which often receives a very happy solution, conforming to the word of God and to sound tradition. May the separated Churches explore together the authentic doctrine of pastoral episcopacy, which would help their unity, as was the case in the Church of the early centuries. Calvin wrote: 'It has long been the case in the Church that the main office of the bishop was to tend the people by God's word or to build up the Church as much in public as in particular by sound doctrine'. How can we not remember here the figure of the patriarch Athenagoras sharing the Gospel with guests and the faithful in his study after the Sunday worship?

9

THE PRESBYTERATE

The presbyteral ministry has three basic characteristics: prophetic, priestly and pastoral. These three characteristics are closely linked in the various presbyteral functions. The pastor has a prophetic ministry in that he is charged with preaching God's word; he has a priestly ministry in that he gives his own life for the faithful and offers them for sanctification by Christ; he has a pastoral ministry in that he exercises the authority of the Spirit to build up the Christian community in unity and love.

The Ministry of the Word and the Sacraments

'Let the elders who rule well be considered worthy of double honour', Paul wrote to Timothy, 'especially those who labour in preaching and teaching' (*en logoi kai didaskaliai*, Tim. 5.17). If he performs his presidential function well, the presbyter is entitled to particular consideration, but the apostle places above all work in the service of the word (*logos*) and of doctrine (*didaskalia*). This dual nature of the presbyteral ministry, prophetic and doctrinal, appears as fundamental and primary. Through the laying on of hands the pastor has received the Spirit of the new Moses, the Christ, who sets him in the new rabbinical succession: the apostolic ministry of the word and of teaching, the prophetic and doctrinal ministry of the new covenant.[6]

In the list of ministries given by St Paul to the Corinthians, there are three that come first as fundamental and primary: 'God has appointed in the church first apostles, second prophets, third teachers, then...' (1 Cor. 12.28). In the list addressed to the Ephesians we find these three ministries again, together with evangelists and pastors who are included among them: 'And (Christ's) gifts were that some should be prophets, some evangelists, some pastors and teachers, to equip the saints for the work of ministry, for building up the body of Christ' (Eph. 4.11–12). We have seen the ministry of the apostle as consisting of arousing faith and founding Churches by witnessing to the risen Lord. This apostolic ministry is essentially the ministry of the word of the eyewitness. After the apostle, the prophet is equally the servant of God's word. His ministry consists of proclaiming that word, based on apostolic witness and moved by the Holy Spirit. As preacher of the evangelistic, apostolic word, the prophet is called to recognize the signs of the times in the light of the Spirit; thus his prophetic word corresponds both to God's word and to the expectations of the world. The teacher (*didaskalos*) is charged with teaching the catechism and doctrine on the basis of God's word. His ministry is to structure the various elements of Christian doctrine to make them into a whole which can be communicated by the catechism. He interprets the teaching of God's word to make it link up with man's life in the world.

Prophet and teacher are conjoined in the presbyter whose ministry is that of the word and of teaching, of prophetic preaching and doctrinal catechism. Based on the evangelistic, apostolic word, he seeks to recognize the signs of the times, to announce God's word in a form of preaching that reaches men today: to this task of preaching is added that of teaching, which presents Christian truth in a way which communicates it to the modern world. This prophetic and doctrinal ministry is basic, for the other forms of the presbyteral ministry depend on it, since this whole ministry is based on God's word and is carried out by means of the word of God. In addressing the elders at Ephesus St Paul urged them to take heed to themselves and to all the flock in which the Holy Spirit had made them overseers to tend God's Church; and this guarding of the flock would consist firstly in doctrinal vigilance, for there would be men who would rise up and speak perverse things in order to draw away the disciples after them. They were to remember the ministry of Paul who for three years did not cease to exhort everyone. He commended them to

God and to the word of his grace, in whose power it was to build them up and to obtain their inheritance with all the sanctified (Acts 20.28–32). It is through God's word, preached prophetically and taught doctrinally, that the presbyter, prophet and teacher can legitimately and assuredly be the shepherd of the flock and pastor of the faithful, and tend God's Church over which the Holy Spirit has made him steward; for God's word alone can build up the Church and transmit the lasting inheritance of the community of the sanctified. Like the pastor, the presbyter is responsible for feeding God's Church, as the shepherd seeks food for his flock; and this food with which he tends the Church is above all the evangelistic and apostolic truth. This prophetic, doctrinal ministry is so essential to the presbyter who is pastor of the Church, that he can cry out with St Paul: 'For if I preach the gospel, that gives me no ground for boasting. For necessity is laid upon me. Woe to me if I do not preach the gospel! For if I do this of my own will, I have a reward; but if not of my own will, I am entrusted with a commission. What then is my reward? Just this: that in my preaching I may make the gospel free of charge, not making full use of my right in the gospel' (1 Cor. 9.16–18). The ministry of preaching and teaching is an invincible necessity for the pastor; the initiative is not his, it is God who has entrusted the commission to him; all his reward lies in this free proclamation of the gospel, renouncing all power and honour, so that only the strength and glory of God alone may be magnified, who speaks through him to men.

This ministry of the word raises new problems today in relation to man's situation in the present world. The pastor, as prophet and teacher, preacher and catechist, must be alert to, and conscious of, these problems concerning the form and content of preaching.

As we have already seen, the pastor may not, any more than any other minister of the Church, be considered a 'sacrificial priest' in the sense of the Old Testament or of human religion. In the light of the New Testament and of the early tradition of the Church, the presbyter or pastor is exercising a new and original ministry in the Church. The word 'priest' should not be used of him, although his ministry may be qualified 'priestly'. We shall see later the significance of this priestly nature of the ministry. And yet, the Church's tradition, as much in the West as in the East, has been orientated towards an idea of the minister as a 'priest', ordained to a 'sacrificial' function which is considered central: the Eucharist. How is this orientation to be explained, and should it be considered a deviation?

The Church's tradition situates God's word in a human, sociological context so that it may be communicated and understood by men at every period in history. This is particularly applicable to the evolution of the form and meanings of the presbyteral ministry in tradition. The basic and essential meaning of the Christian ministry is integrated into a social and religious reality which is modified in the course of history, and allows it to assume varying forms and meanings. These, without betraying the fundamental sense of Christian ministry, at times emphasize one element more than another, or even at the expense of another.

The revolution of the new covenant, concerning the ordained ministry in the people of God lay in the recognition of the end of the sacrificial priesthood of the old covenant, which was fulfilled and completed in the perfect sacrifice of the one high priest, Jesus Christ, and in the substitution on the one hand of a collective priesthood of the whole Church and on the other a particular ministry of servants of the word of God, the sacraments of Christ and the authority of the Spirit. Thus at its beginning the Christian ministry had its socio-religious roots in the institution of presbyters or elders of the Jewish Synagogue rather than in the institution of priests and levites ordained to perform liturgical sacrifices in the Temple. The first Christian presbyters were the successors to the Jewish presbyters who served the word and praise of the Lord, and also the unity of the Synagogue; they were not successors to the priests who carried out the sacrifices and the liturgical rites of the Temple: this sacrificial priesthood found its definitive priest in Christ and was extended to the whole people of God, becoming a priesthood which embraced the whole Christian life, a sacrifice of the bodies of the baptized in praise to God and as a witness to men (Rom. 12.1–2).

But the presbyteral ministry encountered other historical situations. If it was necessary at the beginning for it to be radically distinguished from the sacrificial priesthood, to affirm the uniqueness of the perfection of Christ's priesthood and sacrifice (Hebrews) and also to affirm the universality of the royal priesthood and living sacrifice of the whole Church (1 Peter), this necessity became less acute in the course of the early centuries. In a religious world which had its priests and its sacrifices, like the Greco-Roman world, the Christian presbyters seemed comparable to Christian priests, ordained to eucharistic sacrifice. They did not lose the original character of their ministry dedicated to the good news of Christ, but this was gradually incorporated into an idea of priesthood immediately intelligible to the Gentiles. This had its good and its less good points. The communication of God's word demanded in some way this incorporation of the idea of Christian presbyterate into the priestly and sacrificial culture of the Gentile religious world. But, on the other hand, that incorporation risked overlooking a little the priesthood of all the baptized, from within which God chose servants of this universal priesthood, the Christian ministers. These tended to monopolize the priesthood that belonged to all God's people and, from being ministers ordained to serve the universal priesthood, they became the sole priests of the Church, ordained principally to the sacrifice of the Eucharist, with religious leaders exercising power over the laity. Admittedly this description simplifies the facts, but it was certainly against such priestly and sacrificial power that the Reformation raised its protest, in the name of the universal priesthood and evangelical ministry, which lay in the service of the word and sacraments to feed God's people.

Furthermore, the Reformation in the sixteenth century did not avoid the need to incorporate Christian ministry into a new socio-religious situation. The Reformers challenged the monopoly of the priests by restoring the value of the royal and prophetic priesthood of all the faithful; they sought anew the evangelical originality of the presbyterate as serving God's word, Christ's sacraments and the Spirit's authority. But they were men of the Scripture rediscovered in the original, exegetists, academic teachers and preachers. For them the pastor was above all the servant of God's word, the teacher of the Christian people. Hence the extraordinary importance accorded to expounding the Bible in the pastoral ministry of the Reformed Churches. The supreme Christian worship was no longer the eucharistic sacrifice celebrated by the priest; it tended to become essentially the service of God's word, read **and preached**, accompanied by the praise of psalms and prayers, culminating occasionally in the celebration of the Lord's Supper, the word made visible. The pastor was no longer a priest celebrating a sacrifice, but a teacher proclaiming and expounding the doctrine of Holy Scripture. He discarded the priestly vestments of the liturgy in favour of the academic gown of teaching. Here again we are aware of simplification in this description; distinctions should be drawn: the Lutheran Reformation is distinguished from the Calvinist one in the sense that it was more tolerant of mixing forms and continuing traditions; but basically it arose from the same intention as far as the idea of ministry is concerned. In putting the Christian ministry in its socio-religious context at the time of the sixteenth-century Reformation, there were both virtues and weaknesses. The startling rediscovery of the sovereign authority of God's word contained in Holy Scripture was accompanied by a weakening in sacramental and liturgical life. In the centuries that followed preaching would never lose its importance, even though its style and content varied greatly; but the Eucharist was to be celebrated less and less. That is not to say that the Eucharist is linked to an idea of ministry as sacrificial priestliness, but the teaching and pastoral nature of the Protestant ministry has brought out the role of the word to such an extent that the sense of the sacrament has become blunted, in a sort of imbalance of the various aspects of the Christian ministry.

We are today at the dawn of a new era for the presbyteral or pastoral ministry. Demands born of the secularization of the modern world are forcing the Church to rethink the presbyterate in its sociological context. Today's world no longer knows what a priest or pastor is, nor what is meant by a liturgical sacrifice or a sermon on a sacred text. It is certainly too early to know how the basic Christian ministry will find expression in modern society, without losing any of its originality, while adapting itself to man's conditions today. Above all it is important to distinguish what is specific to the presbyteral ministry, to do some healthy demythologizing to rediscover it in its fundamental intention, in its permanent meaning across the accidents of history. And here we must dwell more particularly on its priestly and sacrificial nature. This is perhaps the most difficult point, and probably the one that has received the greatest variety of interpretations in the course of history, as we have seen.

As we have already said, according to New Testament sources and the early tradition of the Church, we cannot translate 'presbyter' by 'priest', which indicates the minister of the sacrifice in the Old Testament and in the Gentile religious world. But if a presbyter is not a priest, his ministry does have a priestly and sacramental aspect.

The Priesthood of Mission

It is firstly as a member of the people of God that the presbyter or pastor reveals his priestly nature. Like all the laity he belongs to the royal and prophetic priesthood which proclaims God's praises and offers him spiritual sacrifices (1 Pet. 2.9,5). Like all the laity he is called to offer himself as a living sacrifice, holy and acceptable to God (Rom. 12.1). But this royal and prophetic priesthood which offers the body to the sacrifice of God and men he performs not just as a baptized member of the Church, but also as an ordained minister in the Church. His life of service, sacrifice and suffering as a minister of Christ is the prime content of his priestly minister.

It is in the story of the washing of the disciples' feet (John 13) that the pastor reveals the deep and existential meaning of the priestly aspect of his ministry. There Christ shows him that he can only be a sign of his person and action if he makes himself, following his example, the servant of all men. This service (*diakonia*) which is the basic characteristic of the priestly ministry is brought to completion in self-sacrifice. The pastor is a Christian ordained to sacrifice, not in the symbolic or liturgical sense, but in the vital, existential, concrete sense. He gives his life for those whom Christ entrusts to him: he gives generously of his time, his work and leisure. He carries out this self-sacrifice to increase, in the Body of Christ, in the Christian community, in every believer entrusted to him, the sense of the royal and prophetic priesthood, of giving himself to God and to men. He sacrifices himself so that every Christian may be led to this spirit of sacrifice. The priestly aspect of his ministry commits him to a life of service and sacrifice to animate the priesthood of the whole people of God, to make every Christian a priest, a sacrificed servant of God and man. Calvin expressed this sense of the priestly ministry magnificently in a letter to

Farel, written on 24 October, 1540: 'As for my spiritual state, it is this. If I had the choice I would do anything rather than go against your wishes (i.e. to return to Geneva); but as I remember that I am not my own master, I offer my heart, as a slaughtered sacrifice to the Lord'.[7]

This spirit of service and sacrifice of the ministry leads to suffering being welcomed in a priestly perspective. St Paul expressed well this priestly significance of suffering in the ministry. He wrote to the Christians at Colossae: 'Now I rejoice in my sufferings for your sake, and in my flesh I complete what is lacking in Christ's afflictions for the sake of his body, that is, the Church' (Col. 1.24). The apostle does not pretend to complete the redemptive work of Christ by adding his part to that of Christ. He sees the Christian life, and in particular his apostolic life, as conforming to the very existence of Christ. He must live, preach the gospel, serve and suffer, sacrifice himself and die with Christ in communion with him, to come with him to resurrection. The suffering of the Christian, and very particularly that of the apostle or minister, allows him to conform to the suffering of the Crucified and to enter more deeply into communion with him. Thus the apostle's suffering, in his ministry, marks his heart and flesh with the stigmata of Christ's passion. He will always fall far short in his life as a man of attaining that conformity of love and sacrifice with Christ, but he knows that suffering endured because of the gospel he proclaims gradually reduces the distance which separates him from Christ, the perfect suffering servant sacrificed for men. In communion with Christ crucified the apostle's suffering in his ministry becomes suffering for others, for the Body of Christ, for the Church. Indeed, this suffering of the ministry is both a sign bearing witness to the fellowship of the minister with Christ the suffering servant, and a form of his inter-cession for others. Thanks to suffering, which likens him to the Crucified, the minister, through his witness, leads the Christians who are entrusted to him to conform to the mind of Christ (Phil. 2.5): that they should welcome suffering in communion with the suffering Servant. Through his suffer-ing the minister comes very close to Christ in his passion, and this intimacy lends his intercession a new depth and effective-ness: he prays for all men entrusted to him in intimate communion with Christ on the cross, embracing the universe in his outstretched arms. So the primary significance of the priestly aspect of ministry is the spirit of service which leads to sacrifice and makes of the minister a sign of the suffering Servant and an intercessor for the whole Church in the fellowship of the Crucified.

The vocabulary of liturgical sacrifice and sacrifical priesthood is used in the New Testament to express, on the one hand, the gift of a Christian life to the service of Christ and, on the other, the apostolic mission to spread the gospel in the world. The Christian life is seen by Paul as an offering of the whole body as a 'living sacrifice, holy and acceptable to God, which is your spiritual worship' (Rom. 12.1). The gospel mission is equally expressed by St Paul in liturgical and sacrificial vocabulary: '.. the grace given me by God to be a minister of Christ Jesus to the Gentiles in the priestly service of the gospel of God, so that the offering of the Gentiles may be acceptable, sanctified by the Holy Spirit' (Rom. 15.15–16). All the key words in this sentence are taken from the language of the Jewish liturgy: in his apostleship to the Gentiles Paul sees himself as a minister (*leitourgos*) of Jesus Christ, he performs a priestly function (*hierourgon*) with respect to them in proclaiming the gospel, for through this preaching the Gentiles who are converted become an offering (*prosphora*) acceptable to God, being sanctified by the Holy Spirit.[8] The word *prosphora* is used in seven other places in the New Testament, always to indicate a liturgical oblation.

Thus Paul sees his ministry as that of a priest, but not in the Old Testament sense, where priesthood was mainly concerned with the sacrificial liturgy of the Temple at Jerusalem.[9] Paul's liturgy also has a sacrificial aspect: however it does not consist of ritual, propitiatory sacrifices, but in the offering of men to God. Through God's grace and choice the apostle became the minister of Jesus Christ for the nations, that is, all men without distinction; by means of the Holy Spirit he carried out, like a priest, the consecration of an offering acceptable to God, and this new offering was of men who had been converted. The new aspect of this priesthood is that its liturgy implies the proclamation of the gospel and the action of the Spirit, and that its offering is living, made up of men who embrace the Christian faith. The Christian priest and his liturgy no longer have just a ritualistic nature; it is a missionary priesthood and a cosmic liturgy. The Temple is no longer confined to Jerusalem but has been extended to the whole Body of Christ, to the universal Church which must reach all mankind. Christ had already said this to the woman of Samaria: 'Woman, believe me, the hour is coming when neither on this mountain nor in Jerusalem will you worship the Father... the hour is coming, and now is, when the true worshippers will worship the Father in spirit and truth' (John 4.21–23).

Thus the priesthood of the gospel and of the Holy Spirit, as Paul understands it, is essentially a missionary function for offering to God men converted by the gospel and sanctified by the Spirit. This should not be seen as an opposition between mission, the function of preaching, and liturgy, the function of prayer. Mission and liturgy, preaching and prayer, are just a single service in the people of God. But while in Israel it was the sacrificial liturgy of the Temple that basically expressed the existence of the people before God, without excluding mission to other nations, for the Church it is the apostolic mission in the world that defines Christians' existence, the liturgy being the place where the preaching of the gospel is reinforced and where there is gathered the harvest of those who have chosen to follow Christ.

Thus, according to this very important passage in St Paul, ministry is not defined as a liturgical sacrificing, but as an apostolic mission which is understood in liturgical terms. The presbyters or pastors of the Church are no *hiereis*, members of a hierarchy ordained essentially to liturgical and sacrificial celebration, like the priests of the the old covenant, but they are apostles, ambassadors, or missionaries, ministers 'of Christ Jesus to the Gentiles in the priestly service of the gospel of God (*hierourgountes*) so that the offering of the Gentiles may be acceptable' (Rom. 15.16). The use of the active verb *hierourgein* indicates that the function and aim of ministry is to form, together with men converted to Christ, a community priesthood to serve the world. The First Epistle of St Peter explains this fruit of the apostolic ministry thus: 'Like living stones be yourself built into a spiritual house, to be a holy priesthood (*hierateuma hagion*), to offer spiritual sacrifices acceptable to God through Jesus Christ... You are a chosen race, a royal priesthood (*basileion hierateuma*), a holy nation, God's own people, that you may declare the wonderful deeds of him who called you out of darkness into his marvellous light' (1 Pet. 2.5,9). It is the same liturgical language that is used here to express the existence of the community for men. The ambiguity of the words 'wonderful deeds' which translate *aretai* (virtues, praises) shows again here the indissoluble link between witness and prayer, preaching and liturgy. The royal priesthood of all God's people has the basic duty of proclaiming the wonderful deeds of God, which means both announcing the good news of the gospel to the world and performing the act of thanksgiving to God for the gospel, in the liturgy.

The quotation from the Epistle to the Romans (15.16) again illustrates the radical difference between the priesthood in Israel and ministry in the Church; it also shows us how this ministry is deformed when it reverts to the Old Testament idea. The priesthood of Israel was essentially within God's people and for them. Liturgies and sacrifices were offered by the priests exclusively for the Jewish believers. The priest was the property of the people and served them as mediator between God and the faithful. Admittedly the Church's ministry is also for the common priesthood of believers; but this priesthood consists of a mission which is constantly bringing it out of the community into the world, where it seeks out those who are to be called by Christ to a life of faith. The Christian priestly idea of the ministry takes the pastor out of the ecclesiastical framework to send him constantly on mission into the midst of the world. Then he becomes a true mediator between God and men. The missionary priestly vision of St Paul saves the ministry from a sort of clericalization within the ecclesiastical institution. When priesthood is seen only as a function of building up the Church by ritual celebration and doctrinal teaching, it again becomes a priesthood of the old covenant, getting shut in an ecclesiastical ghetto where it becomes stunted and deformed.

Admittedly this function of building up the Christian community is important, but, in the same way as the priesthood of believers is for men and not for the introverted satisfaction of the pious, so the priestly nature of ministry is a constant call to external mission; the royal priesthood of God's people must be built up by the constant addition of new stones which come from outside, it must be made by 'the offering of the nations', by the mission of ministers and the witness of the faithful. That indicates how much the priestly aspect of the pastor obliges him to have unceasing contact with men and with the world; he 'the minister of Jesus Christ for the nations' and not the priest owned by an ecclesiastical community for its own exclusive use in worship or teaching.

The presbyteral ministry and the priestly people of the faithful each carry out according to their function, the missionary liturgy in the new Temple which is Christ's Body spread throughout the world. The pastor, for his part, performs the function of priest through the gospel to offer to God those touched by Christ and sanctified by the Holy Spirit; thus he builds up the priestly community of the faithful which in turn proclaims the wonderful deeds of God, by committed witness in the life of the world and by the active liturgy of thanksgiving and intercession before God. The priestly function of the minister in the world is more a mediation through the gospel which he proclaims explicitly; the priestly function of the believer is more a presence in the world where he spreads the gospel abroad through his own existence. It is a question of emphasis more than of radical difference, for it is obvious that the believer is also led to talk of the gospel, just as it is necessary too for the minister to be caught up in the life of the world.

The Office of Intercession

The pastor, whether responsible for a parish or a chaplaincy, whether he gives all his time to the ministry or follows a trade, has a particular duty in the prayer of the Church. Admittedly, liturgical and personal prayer concerns all God's people, ministers or believers. There is no Christian life or church life without this prayer of the community and of each member of the Body of Christ. Prayer is a responsibility of the whole Church, pastors and laity, but the ministers have in it a particular function by virtue of their calling in the Body of Christ. It is, in fact, as ambassadors of Christ in the people of God, as signs of Christ the high priest and intercessor, that ministers have a particular duty of prayer, praise and intercession.

As ambassadors of God among his people, their mission is not just to transmit his word, but they must also give account to the Lord of their ministry and present to him the needs of the faithful entrusted to them. Their pastoral prayer is their means of telling God the joys and preoccupations of their ministry, of offering for his blessing the people in their care. In this priestly function of prayer, the pastor is in the community a sign of Christ the high priest and intercessor; he brings before God, by the mediation of the Son and in the communion of saints gathered by the Spirit, praise and supplication for all those for whom he is responsible, the Christians and non-Christians who are entrusted to him. His prayer does not replace that of the faithful; he is not the man who prays for those who do not pray; every Christian has a special duty in this ministry of prayer, which cannot be avoided and handed over to the ministers. But the pastor has a particular prayer ministry according to his responsibility in the community, which is that of an ambassador of Christ and a sign of the Son's intercession with the Father.

Here the image of the high priest of the old covenant can throw light on this priestly function of prayer: 'So Aaron shall bear the names of the sons of Israel in the breastpiece of judgment upon his heart, when he goes into the holy place, to bring them to continual remembrance before the Lord' (Exod. 28.29).[10] This liturgical ornament, the breastpiece, was decorated with twelve stones carved as seals: each bore the name of one of the twelve tribes of the people of God. Thus, when the high priest went into the holy place, he bore on his heart a stone for each tribe, whom he exposed, one might say, for the blessing of the Lord. We have there a very fine symbol of priestly intercession. Admittedly it is Christ who performed the function of the high priest in entering the heavenly sanctuary, as the Epistle to the Hebrews tells us, to offer the Father the perpetual intercession formed by his unique sacrifice; but in the Church ministers are signs of the interceding Christ and, united to his priesthood, they share this priesthood of prayer, the action of thanksgiving and intercession, for the members of God's people and those who are entrusted to them. So through the mediation of Christ there may indirectly applied to them this image of the high priest bearing on his heart the weight of the stones covered with the names of the sons of Israel as a memorial before God, a prayer which brings to the Lord a reminder of the faithful.

The great prayer of Christ recorded by St John (17), which is commonly called the 'high priestly prayer', is the supreme example of what the minister's function of intercession in the Church should be. It is obviously first of all a prayer of Christ in his unique priestly office. But here again, by sharing in Christ's priesthood, the minister can make this prayer a model for his own priestly prayer for God's people. There are, in this prayer, three great themes which the minister also makes the subject of his own intercession for Christians and for all mankind: the knowledge of truth, mission in the world and unity in the community.

Like Christ the minister prays first that the believers entrusted to him should have eternal life, that is to say knowledge of the one true God: 'And this is eternal life, that they know thee the only true God, and Jesus Christ whom thou has sent'. The minister consecrates himself so that the faithful might be consecrated in the truth: 'For their sake I consecrate myself, that they also may be consecrated in truth' ... 'Sanctify them in the truth; thy word is truth'. Strong in this truth, Christians are sent out on mission into the world, a world which hates them because they are not of the world: 'I do not pray that thou shouldst take them out of the world, but that thou shouldst keep them from the evil one' ... 'I do not pray for these only, but also for those who believe in me through their word'. But this mission in the world demands the unity of Christians, and the minister with Christ prays too: 'That they may all be one... so that the world may believe that thou hast sent me'. Indeed, if believers argue and are divided how could the world believe in the love of God which should inspire them, how could the world know that God has sent his Son and that he loved men with the very love of God who creates love? Thus the priestly prayer of the minister in the Church, in the image of the prayer of Christ himself, is consecration in the truth of God's word, preparation for mission in the world and consolidation of the unity of the community in Christ and in the communion of saints. These three major themes of the priestly prayer make the minister a man of God's word, when he consecrates himself in truth, a man of intercession, when he prays for all men, and a man of the Eucharist, when he brings together the Christian community in unity.

The minister is firstly a man of God's word, of the Bible, of the truth revealed and lived in the Church. That is the reason why tradition has given him quite particularly a liturgical office through which, either alone or with other believers, he is plunged into God's word to make of it the inspired language of his praise, the privileged place of his fellowship with men, the living food of his meditation. When he says his liturgical office the minister is never alone; if he cannot celebrate it with the community, his praise, intercession and meditation are offered in the name of them all; here he bears the highest burden of his ministry, which is to give a voice and a heart to the unceasing prayer of the Church to its Lord, and to the unknowing aspiration of creation towards its Creator. The Psalms are an important part of this office. In communion with Christ who has prayed them, the minister uses them to translate the praises of creation and of the Church; he is putting himself in the place of those who suffer in body or spirit to express their supplication with them; he turns into benediction the unhearing revolt of men who defy God. In their great spiritual diversity the Psalms enable the minister to make himself everything to all men in his priestly prayer. They have always been an integral part of the office, for they enable men to pray as they would have no idea how to do. Without them prayer would be too individualistic and self-interested; with them the heart can reach out in universal dimensions to the manifold needs of men and especially to the love of Christ who prayed them, and gave them their ultimate meaning in his sacrifice and resurrection.[11] After the praise and supplication of the Psalms the continued reading of Holy Scripture consecrates the minister through truth. In this crucial part of his office of prayer, his heart and spirit are instructed in the thought of the prophets, of Christ and of apostles, with readings from the Church fathers completing this biblical mediation.

We have just outlined the first two parts of every office which conveys the priestly prayer of the minister. In a third part he offers his intercession for the faithful who are entrusted to him and all men whom he meets, in the liturgical intentions and in more personal prayers, naming before God all those for whom he feels moved to pray. He completes this intercession by saying with Christ and the whole Church the Lord's Prayer. The Catholic reform of the breviary, after the Second Vatican Council, has readopted this simple structure of the liturgical office which is indispensable to the renewal of priestly prayer.[12] Several times a day the pastor will stop for this praise, meditation and intercession, to remind himself of his function in the service of God and his people, a function whose most important demand is prayer.

The Eucharist completes this priestly prayer of the minister. As we have seen, this is firstly consecration in the truth of God's word, then intercession preparing for mission in the world; finally it is bringing together the Christian community in unity, so that the world might believe. The Eucharist is this supreme bringing together in unity, since it communicates in a unique way the Body of Christ, the Church, with Christ its head. So it is in the Eucharist that the priestly prayer of the minister will be most intense and that the unity of the community will always be reinvigorated for its mission in the world, which is the main object of the pastor's intercession.

Presiding at the Eucharist

If it is true that the Eucharist is at the centre of the Church's life, it is at the very heart of the presbyteral ministry. Through God's calling, which has set him apart from the people of the baptized, and by the laying on of hands, the pastor has received the gifts of the Spirit to exercise in Christ's name an ambassadorship among men for their reconciliation with God and among themselves: 'We are ambassadors for Christ', Paul wrote to the Corinthians, 'God making his appeal through us. We beseech you on behalf of Christ, be reconciled to God... Working together with him, then, we entreat you not to accept the grace of God in vain' (2 Cor. 5.20–6.1). The pastor acts as an ambassador in Christ's name by preaching God's word and by celebrating the sacraments, with the authority of him who sent him in giving him the Holy Spirit: 'God making his appeal through us'. The pastor needs these gifts and this authority of the Spirit as much to preach God's word as to celebrate the sacraments. Whether he is proclaiming the gospel or presiding at the Eucharist, the pastor is setting to work these gifts of the Holy Spirit which he received by his vocation and his ordination for his ambassadorship in the name of Christ.

Here it is appropriate to set aside two deviations which have affected the Churches in their stance, which has often been polemical, on the subject of ministry. On the one hand Churches of a Catholic type have stressed the sacramental aspect of ministry so much, at times to the detriment of preaching the word of God, that they have put the accent almost exclusively on the power and authority needed to celebrate the Eucharist with validity. Preaching, thought to be of secondary importance, did not create any great problems. It should be noted that the Second Vatican Council has sensibly restored the balance for the Roman Catholic Church in the constitution on the liturgy, *Sacrosanctum Concilium.* On the other hand, Churches of a Protestant type have strongly underlined the role of preaching in the ministry and have insisted on training pastors for this function much more than on preparing them for the sacramental life and for liturgical prayer. As a result there has been a certain disaffection for the Eucharist and little reflection on its link with the ministry. but here too a better balance is being sought in the light of ecumenical dialogue.

As an ambassador for Christ, invested with the authority of his Lord and equipped with the gifts of his Spirit, it is normal that the pastor should preside at the meal to which God invites his people. He is the sign of Christ saying the words that founded the Eucharist: 'This is my body... This is my blood of the new covenant...' These words he repeats and proclaims in the name of Christ. Like an ambassador who hands over his credentials from his government and who is thus the witness of a covenant, the pastor, in the celebration of the Eucharist, transmits the Lord's testament, of which he is the authorized representative, he is the witness of the new covenant proclaimed in the Eucharist, he is the means by which Christ guarantees his promise. The pastor has received the gift to invoke the Holy Creator Spirit, so that the bread and wine of the Lord's Supper may be consecrated and he may fulfil the promise of Christ to have his Church partake of his body and his blood, being truly present in the midst of his people.

As a sign of Christ, the one high priest of the people of God, the pastor has also the responsibility of offering the Father a memorial of the Lord, an active sacrifice of thanksgiving and intercession. In communion with the unique priesthood of Christ, who has offered once for all on the cross and offers continually in heavenly intercession the perfect praise and fervent supplication of God made man, the pastor, taking the eucharistic signs of the presence of the risen Crucified and of the living Intercessor, offers them as a memorial to the Father, to give him thanksgiving and to beg him to grant to all men the rewards of the sacrifice of the Son. In union with the glorious Christ who intercedes with the Father, the pastor offers God the active sacrifice of thanksgiving and intercession of the Church. Just as the Son's perpetual intercession is constituted by the memorial of his unique sacrifice on the cross, so the eucharistic prayer spoken by the pastor takes the form of recalling God's wonderful works which culminate in Christ's offering... 'This is my body which is given for you... This is my blood of the new covenant, shed for you and for many for the remission of sins'.[13]

The role of the pastor in presiding at the eucharistic meal is not then simply a question of organization, but it has a deep theological significance, since there the minister fulfils supremely his function of ambassador of the head of the Church and as the sign of Christ the high priest. Yet, given that, more than anywhere else, Christ takes all the initiative and is everywhere in his real presence, the Eucharist which is the highest function of the ministry is also the place where the minister is the most self-effacing before the action of Christ himself. There is, in the Eucharist, a sort of *kenosis*, an annulment of ministry, before the dazzling light of Christ actually present in the mystery of his death, resurrection and intercession. Here, more than anywhere else, the pastor can say with John the Baptist: 'He must increase, but I must decrease' (John 3.30). This effacing of the ministry before the priesthood of Christ actually present has at times been expressed liturgically by the priest prostrating himself after the prayer of consecration in the West, or at the moment of epiclesis in certain Eastern rites. Thus the celebration of the Eucharist shows the pastor both the highest meaning of his ministry in communion with Christ's priesthood, of which he is the ambassador, sign and instrument, and also the humility of his ministry which ultimately leaves all the room for Christ the one high priest of his people, who is actually present in the signs of his body and blood, in the memorial of his sacrifice and intercession.

By virtue of his vocation and ordination which have given him the spiritual gifts necessary for his function as an ambassador of God, the pastor is therefore the minister of the Eucharist who presides at the feast, invokes the Holy Spirit,

124

repeats the words of Christ and offers the Father the memorial of the cross, resurrection and intercession of the Son, the sacrifice of praise and supplication of the Church.[14] He is not enjoying here a private priestly power; it is as a pastor of the Christian community, surrounded by the faithful and with them, that he performs this ministry of presiding at the Eucharist, and shares in the unique priesthood of Christ. But it is he personally who has received the spiritual gifts in his vocation and ordination, even though he only exercises them in the community of God's people. However small the congregation, even if, exceptionally, he may be celebrating the Eucharist alone, the pastor can only carry out the memorial of Christ in communion with the whole Church. He is still Christ's ambassador to his people and the sign of the head of the Church, of the head of the Body. It is for that purpose that he has received the spiritual gifts of the ministry.

Catholic tradition, which is very rigid concerning priestly power as a condition for sacramental validity, has however conceded that, in an emergency a non-ordained believer may celebrate the sacrament of baptism. We are not concerned here with studying the reasons for extending this possibility. This arrangement is related to a very strict conception of the necessity of baptism for eternal salvation, hence the obligation to accept dispensing with the ministry to celebrate it in cases of extreme urgency, when death is likely. Calvin protested against this practice and was more demanding as to the need for ministry in the celebration of the sacraments: 'It is here also pertinent to observe', he wrote, 'that it is improper for private individuals to take upon themselves the administration of baptism; for it, as well as the dispensation of the Supper, is part of the ministerial office. For Christ did not give command to any men or women whatever to baptize, but to those whom he had appointed apostles. And when, in the administration of the Supper, he ordered his disciples to do what they had seen him do (He having done the part of a legitimate dispenser), he doubtless meant that in this they should imitate his example'.[15] Recent Reformed tradition, in some areas, has been less strict on this point and has foreseen cases of necessity where pastoral delegation to a non-ordained believer could be accepted exceptionally or temporarily, to celebrate the Eucharist. This possibility has at times been thought by Catholics to be current practice in Protestantism. But it must be remembered here that we are dealing with very particular cases, known only in certain areas of the Reformed Church and subject to rigorous ecclesiastical ruling.

Preaching, baptism and the Eucharist together belong to the ordained ministry of the Church, for they are acts which are part of the ambassadorship or mission of the pastors: they show the work of Christ as head of the Church, which is his Body, and the pastors have received the necessary spiritual gifts to be signs of the priesthood of Christ in the people of God. This is the ordinary, normal situation of the ministry of the word and sacraments in the Church. If we need more men in the ministry, out of pastoral and missionary necessity, presbyteral vocation and ordination would not be devalued by increasing the amount of pastoral delegation to the laity of functions belonging to the ministry. Instead we should look at the possibility of developing the diaconate, or even a presbyterate which would be conferred on men doing an ordinary job and spending a limited amount of time working for the Church.

We shall examine further the significance of the diaconate and its ministerial functions in tradtition. Presiding at the celebration of the Eucharist has always been reserved for the bishop or presbyter. The deacon has only had secondary functions. But should it not be possible, in emergencies and in the absence of a pastor, for the authority of the Church to delegate to deacons the function of presiding at the Eucharist?

10

THE DIACONATE

The diaconate is the common subject of research by Churches who have all neglected this ministry and are all in a state of great perplexity. We cannot pretend here to elucidate the problem of the diaconate, which has only just been raised again after the Second Vatican Council. There needs to be time yet for this ministry to find its place again, if this is to be found. Admittedly the Second Vatican Council has established the principle of the permanent diaconate, but its true existence between the presbyterate and the lay ministry raises many questions which could be summed up thus: between the presbyters or pastors, whose social standing can change rapidly, to the extent of allowing some to follow another job, and the laity or believers, whose participation in certain functions of the ministry will be developed, what would be the place of the deacons who, alongside their job, would be committed to certain ministerial duties? Has this position between pastors and believers been reduced to the extent that the existence of a permanent diaconate again becomes very problematic?

The Second Vatican Council has this to say about deacons: 'At a lower level of the hierarchy are deacons, upon whom hands are imposed "not into the priesthood but into a ministry of service"' (*Lumen Gentium* 29). Indeed strengthened by the grace of the sacrament they do serve God's people, together with the bishop and his presbytery in the 'diaconate' of the liturgy, of the word and of charity. According to what competent authority will have assigned him, it pertains to the deacon solemnly to administer baptism, to be custodian and dispenser of the Eucharist, to assist at and bless marriages in the name of the Church, to take the last rites to the dying, to read Holy Scriptures to the faithful, to instruct and exhort the people, to preside at the worship and prayer of the faithful, administer the sacraments and to officiate at funeral and burial services. Given to works of charity and administration, deacons should remember St Polycarp's warning: '(Deacons should be) compassionate, diligent, walking according to the truth of the Lord who became a minister (deacon) of all' (The Epistle of St Polycarp, in Bishop Lightfoot, *The Apostolic Fathers*, p. 178). And as these functions which are most necessary to the Church's life may only be carried out with difficulty in many regions if the present discipline in the Roman Church is observed, the diaconate could in future be restored as a right and proper level in the hierarchy. It is for the various local episcopal assemblies, with the approval of the Supreme Pontiff, to decide if and where it is appropriate, for the good of souls, to institute such deacons. With the Supreme Pontiff's consent this diaconate could be entrusted to mature men, perhaps even already married. and to young men of ability whom the law of celibacy must, however, remain in force.[16]

It is the liturgical function of the deacon which occupies the main place here; the rest of his ministry is not defined. One might legitimately ask whether all the liturgical acts of the diaconate listed here could not be performed by laymen delegated for this purpose, either occasionally or permanently? Before discussing the validity of the diaconate today, it is appropriate to explore a little the early tradition of the Church.[17]

An Opening of the Variety of Ministries

In the New Testament the words *diakonos* (servant), *diakonia* (service) and *diakonein* (to serve) are used in a general sense relating to the service of others, derived from the usual concrete meaning of serving at table (Luke 17.8) or taking care of the needs of a guest (Luke 10.40). A series of references call all kinds of ministry in the Church *diakonia*: the apostolate, prophecy, preaching the gospel, mutual help in material things (Rom. 11.13; 1 Pet. 1.12; 2 Tim. 4.5; Rom.

15.31). The Acts of the Apostles talks of serving at tables and service in the ministry of the word (6.1,2,4): while the apostles continued to devote themselves 'to prayer and the ministry of the word', they ordained seven 'Hellenists' for daily service at tables, for them to join with the 'Hebrews' in giving help to the widows. As we have seen, these were not the first deacons; they were not given the name. However, tradition related very early on the ordination of the seven to the ministry of deacons, who were considered ministers of material charity, of 'serving at tables' in the Church.

The name deacon, in the technical sense of a ministry, appears for the first time at the beginning of the Epistle to the Philippians (between AD 53 and 63): 'Paul and Timothy, servants of Christ Jesus, to all the saints in Christ Jesus who are at Philippi, with the bishops and deacons'. But there is nothing to indicate what sort of function these deacons had. We have to wait for the Pastoral Epistles to have some details, although these relate more to the qualities required of deacons rather than to their specific functions. However, in the light of these diaconal qualities, we can realistically imagine some of their duties. If they must not be 'double tongued ... not greedy for gain' (1 Tim. 3.8) it is likely that they were responsible for managing the Church's possessions. If they had to 'hold the mystery of the faith with a clear conscience' (1 Tim. 3.9) it was because, like the over-seers, they were responsible for preaching God's word. St Ignatius of Antioch, some years later, confirms this hypothesis, charging the deacons with the material help of charity and associating them with the ministry of the word: 'And those likewise who are deacons of the mysteries of Jesus Christ', he wrote to the Trallians. 'must please all men in all ways. For they are not deacons of meats and drinks but servants of the Church of God' (Tral. II). The association between Ignatius's writing and Pauline ideas is clear. Paul wrote of his ministry: 'This is how one should regard us, as servants of Christ and stewards of the mysteries of God' (1 Cor. 4.1). The mystery of the faith (1 Tim. 3.9), the mysteries of God or of Jesus Christ (1 Cor. 4.1; Tral. II) is God's truth and will, expressed in the history of salvation and proclaimed in preaching and in the sacraments. Elsewhere St Ignatius speaks of a deacon, Philo from Cilicia, 'who now also ministereth to me in the word of God' (Phil. XI).

The Epistle to Timothy makes provision for preparing candidates: 'Let them.. be tested first; then if they prove themselves blameless let them serve as deacons' (*diakoneitosan*, 1 Tim. 3.10). There we are really faced with a diaconal institution which includes a probationary period followed by designation or ordination.

Although at the beginning of the second century the function of a deacon does not appear as well defined as that of the overseer or presbyter, the diaconate is already showing some consistent features which are to be found subsequently in tradition; it is a ministry of material charity and of evangelical preaching subject to the episcopate whom it assists in the duty of presiding; it implies training and ordination.

Moreover, women are admitted to the diaconate from the beginnings of the Church. St Paul refers to 'our sister Phoebe, a deaconess of the church at Cenchreae' (Rom. 16.1; the feminine *diakonissa* only appeared in the fourth century). In the first Epistle to Timothy, in the middle of the passage on deacons (1 Tim. 3.8–13) we read this: 'The women likewise must be serious, no slanderers, but temperate, faithful in all things'. The most reliable exegesis sees here women deacons. It cannot mean female Christians in general, in the middle of a discussion of the diaconate. Nor can it be a question of deacons' wives; the text would have said 'their wives'. We can understand why the writer uses the word 'women', because there was no feminine form of *diakonos*; if he wanted to distinguish between male and female deacons the most natural thing would be to co-ordinate the sentences as he does: 'The women likewise...' The role of the widows (1 Tim. 5.3–16) must be distinct from that of the women deacons; the widows formed an ascetic, contemplative community, while the women deacons had a true ministry to perform. The younger Pliny, legate in Bithynia between 111 and 113, refers to them in a letter to Trajan: '(This) made me decide to extract the truth by torture from two slave-women (*ancillae*) whom they call deaconesses (*ministrae*)'.[18] While the order of widows disappeared at the end of the fourth century, the female diaconate continued to develop. The *Apostolic Constitutions* refer to widows and deaconesses, but only the latter receive the laying on of hands: 'O bishop thou shalt lay thy hands upon her in the presence of the presbytery and of the deacons and deaconesses'.. 'A widow is not ordained'.[19] Deaconesses had an active ministry for centuries. Their decline began in the tenth century and they disappeared in the twelfth century.

The somewhat ill-defined nature of the diaconate in early tradition makes it more an opening for the laity to the ordained ministry than a closed, stable and permanent order. The access of women to this ministry, which is surprising at a time when they were held in submission to men, gives the same impression. The diaconate is a sort of bridge between the episcopal or presbyteral ministry and the non-ordained believers; it creates a passage between ministry and laity, the ministry is opened to a variety which the spiritual imagination, faced with pastoral and missionary demands, could develop; it prevents the ministry from becoming clericalized and separated from the people.

St Paul expressed this variety of ministries which really makes the Church appear as a body, and which calls all its members to the 'work of ministry (*ergon diakonias*) for building up the body of Christ' (Eph. 4.12). To the Corinthians Paul writes: 'There are varieties of gifts but the same Spirit; and there are varieties of service (ministries) but the same Lord; and there are varieties of working but it is the same God who inspires them all in every one' (1 Cor.12.4–6). Ministry, like the structure of the Body of Christ, can only be thought of as multiple. Even if there are basic ministries, like the episcopate, the presbyterate and the diaconate, they cannot be considered exclusive. While ministry has a basic three-fold structure, it is multiple in its appearance throughout history, because of the pastoral and missionary needs of the Church. And the diaconate is precisely the fundamental ministry which always breaks out into a great variety, the sign and function of the Church's vitality under the direction of the Spirit, multiplying its gifts.

We see the ministry breaking out in variety from the start of the apostolic Church. 'God has appointed in the church first apostles, second prophets, third teachers, then workers of miracles, then healers, helpers, administrators...' (1 Cor. 12.28). It is a similar open list, after indicating the major ministries, that we find again in the Epistle to the Ephesians: 'And (Christ's) gifts were that some should be apostles, some prophets, some evangelists, some pastors and teachers, to equip the saints for the work of ministry, for building up the body of Christ' (Eph. 4.11–12). St Paul gives first the fundamental ministries of the apostolic age, then the list seems to extend to other functions inspired by the Spirit through charismatic gifts. For the Church at the time of the apostles, there was at first the ministry of the apostles who were still alive, the ministry of the prophets of God's word who prolonged and localized the apostles' ministry, and of the teachers who continued their doctrinal teaching. But the list of ministries is open; it is lengthened under the Spirit's guidance: there are evangelists and pastors, there are the spiritual gifts of healing, material help and church government... When this apostolic list evolved to give way to an ecclesiastical list, after the Pastoral Epistles and St Ignatius, due to the implanting of local churches into the succession of the now dead apostles, the major ministries of the episcopate, presbyterate and diaconate, however fundamental, did not exclude other ministries given by the Spirit, according to the pastoral and missionary needs of the Church.

Since the diaconate was precisely the ministry that spread out and was multiplied into a great variety of forms of service, it is not surprising that its history is less stable and less clearly defined than that of the episcopate or presbyrate. One may wonder if it is possible for the diaconate to be a permanent ministry, as the Second Vatican Council wished. Would it not be right for it to be either a ministry of transition and probation, prior to the presbyteral ministry, or a temporal ministry given to laymen for the duration of a particular form of service? With reference to the diaconate as a transition and probation, one could in fact ask if it would not be normal for the Catholic Church, having ordained married men deacons, to grant them later ordination as priests with a view to a complete ministry. One thinks of Latin America where there is such a shortage of priests and where the problem is not so much to give deacons functions that, theologically, delegated laymen, catechists, could carry out (preaching, catechism, spiritual guidance, baptisms, marriages, burials), but to increase the possibilities of celebrating the Eucharist with a priest presiding. Historically, at least in the West, the diaconate has most often been a ministry of transition and probation, and this is not a deviation; rather, it appears to be the normal consequence of the situation of the diaconate, between the laity and the presbyterate: it is, in fact, a bridge or a passage which recalls the unity of God's people and prevents any barrier or clerical separation between them and the ministry. The mistake in the West is to have submitted this provisional diaconate to clerical conditions, such as celibacy, which prevented the natural return to the state of a laymen if diaconal probation was not decisive. All deacons necessarily became priests; the only free probation, allowing a reversal, was the time in a seminary before the diaconate, marked by minor orders, which had no proper ministerial significance. Happily, postconciliary reform is in the process of re-examining these minor orders which lack any real function.

A Temporary, Permanent or Monastic Diaconate

But if the diaconate can be a ministry of transition and probation with a view to the presbyterate, can it not also be a stable ministry without aiming at the pastorate? Certainly, and tradition is there to provide us with numerous examples. What we can examine is whether the diaconate must be seen as a definite commitment, given its nature as a transition ministry. Just as it can be a stage, a probation which is completed by presbyteral ordination, so it ought also to be a temporary ministry entrusted to laymen for the duration of service to the Church. This is how the sixteenth century Reformed tradition very wisely conceived of it. The Discipline of the French Reformed Churches, along with many others, expresses it thus: 'As for deacons, their duty will be to visit the poor, the prisoners and the sick, and to go into houses to catechize. The office of deacons is not to preach the word, not to administer the sacraments, however much they may help in this; and their duty is not permanent, although neither they nor the elders can relinquish it without the permission of the Churches' (articles 22 and 23)[21] According to the Reformed tradition of the sixteenth century, then, the diaconate is temporarily conferred on a layman; he can relinquish this ministry with the permission of the Churches, or else persevere with it and thus eventually prepare for the pastoral ministry. In this vein the national Synod of Poitiers (10 March 1561) explained thus the articles of Discipline on the diaconate: 'The office of deacon is to collect and distribute money for the poor, the prisoners and the sick and to visit them in their affliction, and to go from house to house catechizing families; and if any of the deacons is adjudged worthy and if he promises to devote his whole life to God's service in the ministry of the gospel, then he may be chosen by the pastor and by the consistory to recite the catechism publicly, according to the form approved in our Churches; and that only to train them, without giving them any power to administer the holy Sacraments'. Thus, according to this Reformed discipline, a layman can become a deacon for a limited time, then resume his place among the believers or, conversely, if he wants a lifelong ministry, be chosen to train within the diaconate for the pastoral ministry which he might receive later. Certain Churches even, as in Switzerland, have only this form of the diaconate which is a preparation for the pastorate with, for example, the following functions: to say matins daily, to preach when a pastor is unable to do so, to baptize infants, bless marriages, visit the sick and assist the pastor at the Lord's Supper.[22] These functions of the deacon were in the line of the universal tradition of the Church.

As the Reformed diaconate was temporary, the liturgy conferring it was an installation and did not include the laying on of hands.[23] In fact, in a general way, Reformed tradition, like Catholic tradition, has linked the laying on of hands for ministry with a definite commitment.

This Reformed conception of the temporary diaconate, the limited ministry of a layman or a ministry preparatory to the pastorate, seems to conform to the very nature of the diaconate, an intermediate church order, opening onto both the presbyterate and the laity. It is perhaps here that we should seek to rediscover a modern diaconate in the service of the Church. The diaconate as a possible provisional stage towards the presbyterate need not detain us here; it is well known in tradition: it would need only slight adaptation to declericalize it, to make it an effective probation of sufficient length, to safeguard the full freedom of returning to being a layman if the trial is inconclusive.

A diaconate of limited duration for a believer who wants to perform a service in the Church without seeking a definitive pastorate, seems to us today an interesting possibility. Besides the growing pastoral and missionary needs, there is the current need to set to work in the ministry as many laymen as possible, to free the pastors from numerous spiritual and material tasks, which, because of their great number and repetitive nature, risk turning them into harassed civil servants of religion. It is also important to declericalize the pastoral ministry by setting it in a working community, where the unity of all the people of God, believers and pastors, and a great variety of the gifts of the Spirit may be manifested without any radical separation of ministers and laity. The temporary deacons would on the one hand share in the charismatic ministry, set aside for the building up the Body of Christ, and on the other share fully with the laity the social status of an ordinary full-time job. As their diaconate would be limited the ministry would not run the risk of cutting them off from the laity whom they would have to rejoin sooner or later. The deacons would be able to establish a constant link between the episcopal and presbyteral pastorate and the laity, of whom they would be members temporarily delegated to the ministry. There we should find put into reality this bridge function which we have noted in the traditional diaconate. Men and women without distinction would have access to this diaconal ministry, conforming with the oldest tradition.[24]

The functions of this modern diaconate may be the same as those foreseen for the traditional diaconal ministry. The deacon is firstly the minister of concrete, material charity and responsible for carrying out brotherly distribution within the Church. As the Reformed discipline foresaw, he has a duty to arouse the generosity of Christians towards each other and towards those in need; he is a sign of the brotherly love and of the communal nature of goods in the Church. He is the supreme minister of the *agape*, of generous and sacrificial charity. Equally he will look after group meetings and meals within the community, love feasts where there can be seen the generosity and sharing of Christians among themselves and with all men. In the line of this ministry of charity, the deacon is also the minister of visits to those who are in need, to the old and the lonely, the sick and the infirm, to prisoners. He brings them the brotherly help of the Church, both material and spiritual.

The deacon also shares in the ministry of God's word and of the sacraments. As we have seen, the reforming ordinances of Basle (15.4.1529) listed the features of the deacon, conforming exactly to Catholic tradition, and these were repeated by the Second Vatican Council. According to this ecumenical tradition it is the deacon's duty:

1. to preside over the prayer and worship of the faithful,
2. to proclaim God's word, in reading the Bible and preaching,
3. to officiate at baptisms,
4. to distribute the Eucharist,
5. to be present at marriages in the name of the Church and to bless them,
6. to officiate at burial services.

The Second Vatican Council also added to these traditional functions: the administration of the last rites to the dying and sacramental rites.[25] To this ministry of the word and of the sacraments would be added that of spiritual guidance. It would in fact be desirable that the diaconate should allow the gifts of understanding and of guiding the Christian life of others to be discerned among the faithful. Equally, some Christian psychologists could find in the diaconate a consecration by the Church of their role which is indispensible to the Christian life.

The spiritual, pastoral and missionary imagination of the Church could find many other uses for this diaconal ministry today.[26] In large city centres or slums, on housing estates, the ministry of the deacons could be to take responsibility for a human group within the Christian community which is sometimes too big to achieve real fellowship. They could give true inspiration to the community life of the Church in a collegiate relationship with the pastors. Sharing the ministry among several allows a return to sources and refreshment which is indispensable to the vitality of the Church. Furthermore, it places personal ministry in a collegiality which responds both to a profound reality of the gospel and to a general aspiration of modern society: Christ instituted not individual apostles, but an apostolic college; the work of modern man — scientific, technological, industrial, commercial, agricultural — is increasingly the work of a team if it is to be effective and fruitful.

There is another area of the Church's life where the diaconate can be placed: the so-called 'religious' communities, either monastic or apostolic. Admittedly these communities are not ministerial by nature, but rather are made up of Christians, laymen or ministers, who have committed themselves by vocation to consecrate themselves unreservedly to Christ. This religious consecration (we use the current term in the absence of a more exact one) is essentially part of the baptismal order, a prolonging and deepening of consecration by baptism; it is a particular manifestation of the royal priesthood of the baptized, it is not ordination to a ministry. That is why the monastic communities were initially lay communities, and why priests who were admitted had no particular prerogatives; they could simply carry out the functions of their ministry to serve the community. It was only in the Middle Ages that the custom grew up in the monasteries of ordaining to the priesthood monks consecrated to the prayer of the chanted office, while the lay brothers, responsible for material tasks, remained ordained. This abnormal division into two classes is today in the process of disappearing. The priesthood, and especially the celebration of the Eucharist, appeared to be the culmination of a monk's praise. The custom of private masses probably favoured this spirituality of the monastic priesthood. The religious of apostolic communities followed the same pattern as the monks in this spirituality of the eucharistic priesthood; yet for them the apostolate made presbyteral ministry often more necessary than for the monk.

It it is true that the religious life does not necessarily imply presbyteral ordination, monks or non-ordained religious could not simply be assimilated to the laity in the Church. It would be yet another medieval legal concept to say that those who are not priests are laymen. Because they are consecrated to praise and serve Christ in the spirit of poverty, in the chastity of celibacy and in the obedience of community life, monks and religious, without necessarily being presbyters, are nonetheless committed to a permanent ministry, a diaconate of prayer, hospitality, spiritual guidance and evangelism...[27] Their life and work correspond to a particular diaconate in the service of Christ and the Church. So should they not receive diaconal ordination which consecrates them to their usual ministry? Some of them could receive presbyteral ordination for the needs of the ministry, but most would be deacons. This ministerial title would moreover befit their lives consecrated to the service of Christ, the Church and mankind, in generosity and sacrifice. Similarly, women in religious communities could receive diaconal ordination. This monastic or religious diaconate would obviously have a permanent and definitive character, corresponding to the perpetuity of the commitment of the community. Diaconal ordination could even be administered in the liturgy of the solemn profession by which the members of the community commit themselves definitively.

As we have seen, the celebration of the eucharist has an important place in monastic consecration and praise. Could not the authority of the Church grant deaconmonks the possibility of presiding at the Eucharist?

PART FOUR

ORDINATION TO THE MINISTRY

11

ORDINATION IN THE EARLY CHURCH

Four passages in the New Testament give an indication of an act of the laying on of hands with the explicit meaning of ordination to the ministry.

(a) The Twelve said to the disciples: 'Therefore, brethren, pick out from among you seven men of good repute, full of the Spirit and of wisdom, whom we may appoint to this duty (serving tables)... These they set before the apostles and they prayed and laid their hands upon them... And Stephen, full of grace and power, did great wonders and signs among the people (Acts 6.3,6,8).

(b) 'Now in the Church at Antioch there were prophets and teachers... While they were worshipping the Lord and fasting, the Holy Spirit said: "Set apart for me Barnabas and Saul for the work to which I have called them". Then after fasting and praying they laid their hands on them and sent them off. So, being sent out by the Holy Spirit, they went down to Seleucia: and from there they sailed to Cyprus' (Acts 13.1,2–4).

(c) 'Do not neglect the gift which you have (Timothy), which was given you by prophetic utterence when the council of elders laid their hands upon you' (1 Tim. 4.14).

(d) 'Hence I remind you (Timothy) to rekindle the gift of God that is within you through the laying on of my hands; for God did not give us a spirit of timidity but a spirit of power and love and self-control' (2 Tim. 1.6–7).

From these passages emerge the following characteristics which throw some light on the doctrine of ordination:

1. *The Holy Spirit is both the master of, and the criterion for, choice by the Church of candidates for ordination.*

In the case of the seven, the disciples had to choose men 'full of the Spirit and of wisdom' to set before the apostles. In the case of Barnabas and Paul it was the Spirit who was expressing himself, probably through the inspiration of the prophets and doctors of Antioch: 'Set apart for me Barnabas and Saul...' Similarly in the case of Timothy, there had been an indication of the Spirit 'by prophetic utterance', that is by the word of the prophets of the Church who were enlightened by the Holy Spirit.

2. *Responsibility for ordination rests with ministers of authority in the Church*

The seven, chosen on the orders of the apostles, were presented to them by the community to receive ordination. Barnabas and Paul were ordained by the prophets and teachers of the Church of Antioch. Timothy received ordination at the hands of Paul and from the college of presbyters.[1]

3. *The act of ordination of prayer and the laying on of hands*

In the case of the ordination at Antioch fasting was added to prayer and the laying on of hands. Fasting here shows the intensity of prayer and of the desire to be totally open to the Spirit's direction. Another passage which we have not mentioned, because there is no explicit laying on of hands, also refers to fasting accompanying prayer in the choice of ministers: 'And when (Paul and Barnabas) had appointed elders for them in every Church with prayer and fasting, they committed them to the Lord in whom they believed' (Acts 14.13). The verb *cheirtonein*, 'to indicate with the hand', later became a technical term of ordination. In Judaism, in the post-exilic period, one became an elder by the laying on of hands by the elders; at the time of Jesus their number was fixed at three. This would show that it was completely normal that any institution of Christian ministers, in the apostolic age, was performed by the laying on of hands, even if that is not explicitly indicated in a story. The mention of choice by prayer and fasting and especially the expression 'they committed them to the Lord' reveals all the spiritual content of the laying on of hands. If one or other element of ordination is missing in a story, it must not be assumed to be of secondary importance. It is rather that for the apostles' contemporaries the various elements used in the ordination of ministers were well known, because they were the same as in the designation of the Jewish elders; there was no point in listing them every time. These elements are, then: prayer with fasting and the laying on of hands; fasting is part of prayer: it is the concrete sign of its intensity. Prayer with fasting is therefore a fervent invoking of the Holy Spirit and the laying on of hands is the visible sign which transmits the spiritual gift of the ministry and commits the new minister to the Lord to consecrate him and entrust him to the Lord.[2]

4. *The fruit of ordination is the spiritual gift of the ministry*

After his ordination by the seven, Stephen was 'full of grace and power'; he did great wonders and signs among the people'. Barnabas and Paul were 'sent out by the Holy Spirit' and they went out on their great mission among the Gentiles. In Timothy was 'the gift of God', which he was not to neglect but to rekindle, to complete the whole ministry that Paul had entrusted to him, for God had given him 'the spirit of power (*dumamis*) and self-control'.

So this ordination by prayer with fasting and the laying on of hands is of Judaic origin: the elders of the Synagogue were ordained in this way by a college of elders. But if the Jewish Synagogue gave the Christian Church its form of ordination to the ministry, it was Christ who gave ordination its deep meaning by giving the apostles charge over the Church.

As we have seen, the Johannine account of the washing of the disciples' feet gives the apostolic mission, and consequently ministerial ordination, its theological and profound significance. The climax of the story is Christ's irrefutable speech:

> 'Truly, truly, I say unto you, he who receives any one whom I send receives me; and he who receives me receives him who sent me' (John 13.20)

Ministry comes from Christ who sends, as the Father sent him into the world, and whoever receives the minister sent by Christ receives Christ himself and the Father who is the source of all mission for the world's salvation. But there is a condition so that the minister who is sent may thus be the sign of Christ clad in his authority: 'If I then, your Lord and Teacher, have washed your feet', said Christ, 'you also ought to wash one another's feet. For I have given you an example, that you also should do as I have done to you' (John 13.14–15). A minister is only clad in the authority of Christ if he shares fully his human condition of a servant in humility.

> 'Truly, truly I say to you, a servant is not greater than his master; nor is he who is sent (*apostlos*) greater than he who sent him. If you know these things, blessed are you if you do them' (John 13.16–17).

In this solemn speech Christ insists on communion between the Lord who sends and the servant who is sent: this communion in authority is achieved if the minister who is sent shares the humility and service of the Lord. Peter and the apostles and the ministers of the Church could only share Christ's mission and authority if they accepted that the Lord is the servant of his people, and, following his example, accepted being servants of others. Then they could base their ministry on Christ's promise: 'He who receives any one whom I send receives me' (John 13.20). The washing of the disciples' feet can rightly be considered as the ordination of the apostles by Christ, ordination to the service of others in humility and to ministerial authority in the name of Christ the servant.

Another Johannine story explains the meaning of ministerial ordination — the commission to forgive sins which the risen Lord gave to the apostles: 'As the Father has sent me, even so I send you' (John. 20.21). Then he breathed on them to give them a physical sign of the gift of the Holy Spirit which they received with the Son's commission in the Father's name and added:

> 'Receive the Holy Spirit:
> If you forgive the sins of any, they are forgiven; if you retain the sins of any, they are retained (John 20.22–23).

Here the risen Lord explains the ministerial authority which was given to the apostles when he washed their feet. That authority was not a personal or independent power which could be exercised at will by the minister. It was the very authority of the gospel which frees mankind. Ministerial authority, which is humble service, lies in freeing man from sin by the word of God. In proclaiming this word the minister is truly clad in the authority of Christ by the power of the Spirit, he is his ambassador, his plenipotentiary minister: the sins he forgives are really forgiven. Like the apostle, the minister, sent by Christ, has received the gift of the Holy Spirit by the laying on of hands, the sign of the gift of the Spirit, like the breath of the risen Lord, and this gift confers on him Christ's authority to forgive sins.

These New Testament passages, the two Johannine stories and those which recount an act of the laying on of hands for ministry, are sufficiently explicit to give solid foundation to the doctrine and practice of ordination in the Church.

At the beginning of the third century, in the *Apostolic Tradition* by Hippolytus of Rome, we see that this New Testament doctrine and practice have not changed; the continuity is obvious. The only place where there seems to be a difference is that while the New Testament seems to be preoccupied with establishing a parallel between the Old Testament priesthood and the ministry of the Church, Hippolytus's text sees a continuity in God's intention which has given on the one hand the Temple its priests and Moses his elders, and on the other the Church its bishops and presbyters. But this comparison must be fully understood. The bishops are not the successors to the elders, the assistants of Moses or heads of the Synagogue. The continuity does not lie in ministers having a similar or analogous function, but in the intention of the love of God not wishing to leave sanctuary (his temple or Church) without service or ministry, as Hippolytus says: *'sanctum tuum sine ministerio non derelinquens'.*[3] In the first century it was not helpful to underline this continuity. Indeed, it was even preferable to indicate a break between the Jewish priesthood and the Christian ministry. However, it must be remembered that the apostles did not hesitate to adopt the presbyteral system of the Synagogue for ruling the local churches. A century later the circumstances were different. There could be an apologetic value in showing that the Church was not without a ministry, and that, like Israel, and even like pagan religions, it has its 'priesthood', which was the perfect priesthood of Christ, shared by ministers, in accordance with the continuing intention of God, who did not leave his sanctuary without service. But, it must be stressed, this continuity, according to Hippolytus, is set in God's merciful intention and not in the nature and function of ministry.

The prayer for laying hands on a bishop in Hippolytus's work is very interesting for what it tells us about the doctrine

of ordination at the beginning of the third century. According
to Hippolytus, the bishop is chosen by the whole people. The
people assembled on a Sunday together with the presbyteral
college and the bishops. Only the bishops laid hands on the
one who was newly elected. 'Let all be silent and pray in their
hearts for the descent of the Holy Spirit'. Then one of the
bishops laid his hands on him while saying the ordination
prayer. So there were two instances of the laying on of hands,
one of them in silence by all the bishops present, calling upon
the Holy Spirit in their hearts, and the other by a single
bishop, who spoke aloud a prayer which gave meaning to the
ordination:[4]

> 'God and Father of our Lord Jesus Christ,
> Father of all mercies and God of all comfort,
> who dwellest on high yet hath respect to the lowly,
> who knowest all things before they come to pass.
> Thou hast appointed the borders of thy Church by the
>   word of thy grace,
> Predestining from the beginning the righteous race of
>   Abraham.
> And making them princes and priests
> And leaving not thy sanctuary without a ministry,
> thou hast from the beginning of the world been well
>   pleased to be glorified among those whom thou hast
>   chosen.
> Pour forth now that power, which is thine, of thy royal
>   Spirit
> which thou gavest to thy beloved Servant Jesus Christ,
> which he bestowed on his holy apostles,
> who established the church in every place, the church
>   which thou hast sanctified into unceasing glory and
>   praise of thy name.
> Thou who knowest the hearts of all,
> grant to this thy servant, whom thou hast chosen to be
>   bishop,
> to feed thy holy flock
> and to serve as thy high priest without blame,
> ministering night and day;
> to propitiate thy countenance without ceasing and to offer
>   thee the gifts of thy holy church.
> And by the Spirit of high-priesthood,

to have authority to remit sins according to thy
  commandment,
to assign the lots according to thy precept,
to loose every bond according to the authority which thou
  gavest to thy apostles,
and to please thee in meekness and purity of heart,
offering to thee an odour of sweet savour.
Through thy Servant Jesus Christ our Lord,
through whom be to thee glory, might, honour
with the Holy Spirit
both now and always and world without end. Amen.'

This prayer of the ordination of bishops has kept its theological value and its authority. It is striking to note that the Roman Catholic Church, after its postconciliary liturgical reform, readopted in its entirety this prayer for the ordination of bishops.[5] This prayer set in the tradition which begins in the New Testament, especially in the Pastoral Epistles, and, through St Ignatius of Antioch, reaches the third-century Church without alteration. This text has remained in use to the present day in the Coptic and Western Syrian liturgies in a fuller form.[6] It is essential to study this prayer if one is to understand the ecumenical Christian doctrine of ordination to the ministry.

The prayer begins with an invocation firmly in the style of Judeo-Christian tradition and interwoven with biblical allusions: the blessing of 2 Cor. 1.3, Psa. 113.5–6, and Suzannah's prayer in the Apocryphal Daniel 13.42. But there appears to be more than a laudatory intention; these texts are chosen because of the spirit that is sought for this ordination. The ministry indeed lies in seeking the Lord's mercy and consolation; the Father is alert to the humble human condition which he wants to help through the ministry; God knows the secrets of hearts and he anticipates the Church's intention by the vocation he gives to its ministers.

God has given rules for the building up of his Church and these rules have been handed down by 'the word of his grace'. This expression is used by St Luke of Christ's preaching or that of his apostles (Luke 4.22; Acts 14.3; 20.32). The ministerial organization of the Church goes back to the word of grace preached by Christ and then by the apostles. It is not just part of ecclesiastical tradition, but is rooted in the revelation of God's word. It is because there exists a revealed ecclesiology that the Church can draw up rules on the basis of fundamental precepts of the ministry as laid down in the New Testament.

Next, the prayer looks at God's faithfulness in the history of salvation: he predestined the righteous race, the descendants of Abraham, and among them he instituted princes and priests, so as not to leave this temple without a liturgy, without service, without ministry (*aliturgical*), since from the moment of creation he wished to be glorified by those he had chosen. The verb 'to appoint', *kathistanai*, *constituere*, indicates an act of God himself, giving ministers to his people. It is used in this sense in several places in the New Testament. For the writer to the Hebrews Christ the Great High Priest is 'appointed (*kathistatai*) to act on behalf of men in relation to God' (Heb. 5.1). The apostles appointed the seven in their office (*katastesomen*, Titus 1.5). In continuing his plan not to leave his sanctuary without ministry, God chooses and appoints, in the Body of Christ, the new Temple, the ministers needed to serve his glory and his people.

After recalling these perspectives of the history of salvation, the prayer invokes the Holy Spirit, epiclesis, on the one chosen by God for the episcopate. It is the Spirit which the Father gave the apostles for them to build up the Church in place of the Temple, so that in the continuation of his plan, God's glory might be perpetually proclaimed by the praise of his Name. This epiclesis asks God to 'pour forth the power' which comes from him. This verb 'pour forth' evokes the oil used to anoint priests in the Old Testament. In the Church this oil of anointing is replaced by the Holy Spirit himself. The sign of the laying on of hands replaces the symbol of anointing in the very act of ordination, when the Spirit is 'poured forth' on the minister. This outpouring of the Spirit is characterised as a power (*dunamis*). In the New Testament the 'power of the Spirit' is related to ministry and mission. Thus Christ receives the power of the Spirit for his messianic mission; after his baptism and temptation 'Jesus returned in the power of the Spirit into Galilee' (Luke 4.14); it was then that his ministry began at Nazareth. Christ was to warn the apostles of the events of Pentecost in these words: 'You shall receive power when the Holy Spirit has come upon you; and you shall be my witnesses in Jerusalem and in all Judea and

Samaria and to the end of the earth' (Acts 1.8); the power of the Holy Spirit conferred ministry and mission on the apostles in the name of Christ.

Thus the prayer of Hippolytus follows a very clear New Testament pattern. The power of the Spirit which was given by the Father to the Son, for his messianic mission, then passed on by Christ to the apostles, for their evangelistic mission throughout the world, is received in turn by the new bishop in the laying on of hands. He is linked to Christ's baptism and to Pentecost, he receives the prophetic gift of the Spirit to proclaim the same message as Christ and the apostles in the power of the Holy Spirit. Between invoking the Spirit and listing the gifts of ministry which are requested, a linking formula recalls the prayer at the election of Matthias: 'Lord, *who knowest the hearts* of all men, show us which... *thou hast chosen* to take the place *in this ministry and apostleship* from which Judas turned aside' (Acts 1.24–25). The prayer of Hippolytus puts it thus: '(Father) *who knowest the hearts of all*, grant to this thy servant, whom *thou hast chosen to be bishop...*' This literary association indicates two aspects of this episcopal ordination. First of all the Church submits to the judgement of God who alone knows the hearts of all men: it is he who has chosen and called this new minister, it is he who ordains him. Further, episcopal ordination is related to the election of Matthias who, by God's choice, was introduced into the college of apostles: the bishop, in turn, is associated with the apostolic college.[7]

Then epiclesis develops by specifying the gifts of the Spirit requested for the bishop; in the laying on of hands the Church makes clear what is expected from the Holy Spirit for the minister being ordained; the gifts invoked are not the same for bishop, presbyter or deacon. In this prayer of Hippolytus the gifts of the Spirit requested through epiclesis on the bishop clearly define his basic charge, which is changeless throughout history, whatever the sociological structures that the episcopate slips into.

1. The first gift of the Spirit requested for the bishop is *pastoral grace*. He is the supreme pastor, following the example of the Good Shepherd giving his life for his sheep. 'Grant to this thy servant chosen by God, as one who serves his brethren according to Christ's example, without being domineering, that the bishop receives the gift of pastoral grace (cf. 1 Pet. 5.2–4).

2. The bishop will have to exercise the sovereign priesthood blamelessly before God, serving him day and night; in union with Christ the intercessor, he will carry out *the priesthood of prayer and praise*. As we have seen, Christ alone is fully entitled to be called Great High Priest. The bishop in his life of prayer and praise, shows in the midst of the Church the unique priesthood of Christ: he is a sign of Christ the Priest before the Father, and head of his Body, the Church. To be this sign of Christ the Priest, praising and prayer to the Father, the bishop must worship God (*leitourgounta*) day and night; he is the man of prayer, the minister of the Christian people to lead them to the act of thanksgiving and intercession. Invoking the Spirit upon the bishop creates a close link between the pastoral and contemplative or liturgical functions.

3. This episcopal function of prayer consists firstly of constantly seeking mercy before the face of God. The bishop, a pastor, has compassion on all the weakness and misery of men. Far from judging, he intercedes primarily for God's mercy on sinners, at one with Christ who 'always lives to make intercession for them' (Heb. 7.25). Secondly this function of prayer lies in offering the gifts of the holy Church. This expression implies the sacrifice of praise through which is offered to God the act of thanksgiving for all his blessings. Here again the bishop is at the head of the Church to pronounce the act of thanksgiving, to offer the sacrifice of praise. Seeking God's mercy and praising him for his goodness find their perfect expression in the Eucharist, the sacrifice of intercession and act of thanksgiving. It is certain that the liturgical terms of this sentence (*hilaskesthai*, *prospherein*) evoke *the Eucharist at which the bishop is the supreme president and celebrant*. It is there that he carries out to the full his function of prayer and praise, seeking the Father's mercy, by the blood of Christ 'shed for many for the forgiveness of sins', and offering the act of thanksgiving for all God's blessings.[8]

4. After alluding to the Eucharist, the ordination prayer asks for the bishop the power to *forgive sins*, according to Christ's command and through the Spirit of the sovereign priesthood. Jesus gave his disciples this power that he had (Matt. 9.6; John 20.23) and the Church in turn asks God to give it to the bishop who is associated with the apostolic

college. It is the Holy Spirit who unites the bishop to Christ's sovereign priesthood, to enable him to exercise this ministry of forgiveness: 'Receive the Holy Spirit. If you forgive the sins of any, they are forgiven' (John 20.22–23).

5. Again the bishop receives the *gift of distributing the gifts of his Church* according to God's command. He is responsible for the organization of ministries desired by God. He will not only be a good administrator, but he will have the gift of discerning men's hearts, to put each to work in the Church, to distribute duties and to ordain those whom he considers fit for ministry and in whom he recognizes God's call.

6. Through the Spirit he receives too *the power to loose all bonds*, like the apostles. This refers to Christ's promise: 'Whatever you bind on earth shall be bound in heaven, and whatever you loose on earth shall be loosed in heaven' (Matt. 18.18). This is not a repetition of what has been said above about the power to forgive sins. The power to loose (as in Matt. 18.18) is more extensive than that of forgiving sins (as in John 20.23). It is a proclamation of Christian liberty given by the Gospel. In announcing the good news of the freedom Christ grants to all who follow him, the bishop is the minister of liberation: he looses man from bondage that denies his calling as a son of God. Through this power to loose in the name of the Gospel, the bishop becomes a champion of all liberty ordained for man's advancement and for his fulfilment in the fellowship of Christ.

7. Finally, the whole ministry of the bishop is summed up in the final request: that God may be pleased *in meekness and purity of heart, offering an odour of sweet savour*. This last biblical expression evokes spiritual sacrifice in union with that of Christ who lived and gave himself 'a fragrant offering and sacrifice to God' (Eph. 5.2). The bishop will be a true sign of Christ if he offers himself to God and to the service of all men in a constant effort of meekness and purity of heart. It is in thus sacrificing himself generously for others that he will be an authentic ambassador for Christ to build up the Church to the glory of God.

We have concentrated on this third-century prayer of the ordination of bishops at some length, because it expresses in a complete way all the functions of ministry in general. The prayer of Hippolytus for the ordination of presbyters adds little else that is new: they are considered as the bishop's assistants in ruling the Church, like the elders chosen by Moses and filled with the Spirit to help him.[9] In the prayer for deacons it is particularly the idea of service that is underlined.[10] In Hippolytus, as in the whole of early tradition, it is the bishop in particular who represents the doctrinal richness of ministry; presbyters and deacons, for their part, have a share in this fullness. So it is understandable that at the Reformation the pastoral ministry took its inspiration more from the episcopate of the early Church than from the presbyterate.

12

TOWARDS AN ECUMENICAL CONCEPTION OF ORDINATION

For Calvin, ordination had a distinctly sacramental nature. In the chapter of the *Christian Institutes* dealing with ministries, a paragraph in the ordination ceremony shows us the meaning he gave it. Basing his argument on Jewish practice, which was adopted by Christ and the apostles, Calvin saw laying hands on new pastors as an action of benediction, consecration and offering:

'It is certain, that when the apostles appointed any one to the ministry, they used no other ceremony than the laying on of hands, in a manner *presented to God* whatever they wished to be *blessed and consecrated...* With the same intent (as I imagine), the Jews, according to the injunction of the law, laid hands upon *their sacrifices:* Wherefore, the apostles, by the laying on of hands, intimated that they *made an offering to God* of him whom they admitted to the ministry... In this way they consecrated pastors and teachers; in this way they consecrated deacons. But though there is no fixed precept concerning the laying on of hands, yet as we see that it was uniformly observed by the apostles, this careful observance ought to be regarded by us in the light of a precept. And it is certainly useful, that by such a symbol the dignity of the ministry should be commended to the people, and he who is ordained, reminded that he is no longer his own, but is *bound in service* to God and the Church.[11]

The words which we have italicized in this extract show that Calvin stresses the fact that the laying on of hands is essentially a sign of offering the new minister to God for his consecration: he is presented to God to be blessed and consecrated, he is offered to him as a sacrifice, and dedicated to his service and to that of the Church. Moreover, because it was the habitual practice of the apostles, the laying on of hands becomes a precept for the Church. Equally, this action stresses the importance of the ministry, or, in Calvin's somewhat emphatic terms, 'the dignity of the ministry should be commended to the people'.

Three times elsewhere Calvin affirms the sacramental nature of the laying on of hands at ordination. In the paragraph where he deals with the sacramental nature of the laying on of hands at ordination. In the paragraph where he deals with the sacraments of the Old and New Testaments, having cited baptism and the Lord's Supper, he writes:

'I speak of those (sacraments) which were instituted for the use of the whole Church, For *the laying on of hands*, by which the ministers of the Church are initiated into their office, though *I have no objection to its being called a sacrament*, I do not number it among ordinary sacraments. The place to be assigned to the other commonly reputed sacraments we shall see by-and-by'.[12]

Here Calvin, recognizing three sacraments, baptism, the Lord's Supper and the laying on of hands, leaves the first two aside, for they are common to the whole Church, given to everyone, while ordination only concerns one category of Christians, the ministers or pastors. It is a distinction that tradition was already making, viewing baptism and the Eucharist as major sacraments. The last sentence refers to Calvin's chapter headed 'The five sacraments falsely so-called. Their spuriousness proved and their true character explained', i.e. confirmation, confession, extreme unction, holy orders and marriage. This chapter XIX is very polemical and particularly attacks external forms rather than the real content of the sacraments of the Roman Church. But one might well think that there is a contradiction in Calvin's argument, since, on the one hand he is calling the laying on of hands a sacrament, and on the other he criticizes the sacramental nature of Roman Catholic ordination. In reality, his criticism relates particularly to the seven degrees of order and the subsidiary ceremonies accompanying ordination to the priesthood. For in the course of his criticism Calvin twice acknowledges the laying on of hands as an authentic apostolic act which he recognizes as sacramental:

'In regard to the true office of presbyter, which was recommended to us by the lips of Christ, I willingly give it that place (i.e. of a sacrament). For in it there is a ceremony (i.e. the laying on of hands) which, first, is taken from the Scriptures; and, secondly, is declared by Paul to be not empty or superfluous but to be a faithful symbol of spiritual grace (1 Tim. 4.14). My reason for not giving a place to the third is because it is not ordinary or common to all believers, but is a special rite for a certain function'.[13]

Baptism and the Lord's Supper are sacraments which are ordinary or common to all believers; the laying on of hands is a particular sacrament, pertaining to ministers alone. Calvin is still making the same distinction here, but without in any way diminishing the sacramental nature of the action. The laying on of hands is a sacrament because it is a *sign of the spiritual grace of God, taken from the Scriptures*. It completely fulfils the dual definition of a sacrament which he gives in a line from St Augustine: '(A sacrament) is an external sign, by which the Lord seals on our consciences his promises of good will towards us... a testimony of the divine favour toward us, confirmed by an external sign... You may make your choice of these definitions, which in meaning differ not from that of Augustine, which defines a sacrament to be a visible sign of a sacred thing, or a visible form of an invisible grace'.[14]

Note again that in his writing Calvin does not hesitate to call pastors 'true priests and ministers of the Church'; through the laying on of hands they enter a truly ministerial 'state'. Calvin distinguishes their ordination, which comes from Christ through the sacrament of the laying on of hands, from the ecclesiastical orders of the Roman Church of his time, which were conferred in complex, non-apostolic ceremonies. His criticism of 'the romanist priests' is violent and unjust: he sees them above all in their function of 'sacrificing' by 'daily immolations'. But this summary criticism gives him the chance to bring out the meaning of ordination and ministry. Pastors are ordained out of the mouth of Jesus Christ to proclaim the gospel and administer the sacraments (Matt. 28.19; Mark 16.15; John 21.15). They are commanded to preach the gospel and tend Christ's flock. He promises them the gifts of the Holy Spirit to have due authority over the Church (Acts 1.8). The four biblical quotations underlying this all concern the mission Christ entrusted to his apostles; Calvin applies these verses to the pastors of the Church, because they are for him the apostles' successors, with the same mission of Christ and the same power of the Spirit: 'You shall receive power when the Holy Spirit has come upon you; and you shall be my witnesses...' (Acts 1.8). Pastors, the inheritors of the apostles' mission, are therefore ordained by Christ himself, through the sacrament of the laying on of hands, to be ministers of the Gospel and the sacraments, to tend Christ's flock and to govern the Church; for this they are given the promise of the gifts of the Holy Spirit. Such is Calvin's very clear teaching concerning ordination. Having criticized certain non-apostolic ceremonies, Calvin states a third time his conviction concerning the sacramental nature of ordination: 'There remains the laying on of hands, which I admit to be a sacrament in true and legitimate ordination'.[15]

This sacramental conception of ordination was not always maintained so clearly in Reformed tradition. Calvin's distinction between the common sacraments of baptism and the Lord's Supper, and the particular sacrament of the laying on of hands was not preserved without modification; the sacramental conception of ordination was allowed to be weakened, while retaining the act of the laying on of hands and its deep significance. At times the polemical opposition to Catholic priesthood prevailed over an ecumenical view of ministry which would have given more depth to Calvin's sacramental conception. In the seventeenth century Reformed theologians were reluctant to talk of the laying on of hands as a sacrament, but one can imagine that this was above all a problem of theological vocabulary. In general they would actually give sacramental meaning to an action that they dared not call a sacrament. Thus Jean Daillé could say, in a sermon on the Second Epistle to Timothy: 'The hand of the Minister was the sign of God's hand, that is of the efficacy of his power; and the Minister laying his hand on someone meant that God was extending his own hand to communicate to him the very gifts necessary for the work for which the Minister was preparing and consecrating him'.[16] It is clearly Calvin's sacramental conception that we see again here. A specialist on the ministry in the seventeenth century has summed up the Reformed doctrine of the time as follows:

'Like the two sacraments, the laying on of hands comes to bear witness to, and authenticate for the minister and his people, the promise which God makes in his word. It signifies both a definitive consecration of the man who is now committed to the ministry for life and the acknowledgement that he has henceforth in the Church a special place insofar as he must guide and feed the people entrusted to him in God's name'.[17]

Thereafter the doctrine of ordination does not change much in the genuine Reformation tradition. The liturgy of the ordination of Reformed and Lutheran pastors in France expresses the common doctrine very clearly. This is the first part of the prayer which accompanies the laying on of hands and forms the central part of the ordination:

'Let us pray.
The candidate kneels.
The congregation kneel or bow their heads.
Lord God, heavenly Father, we give you thanks for the work of your Son, Jesus Christ, for his redeeming death, his resurrection and his ascension into glory. He it is who, by the Holy Spirit, has raised up apostles, evangelists and witnesses and who, down the ages, has given to the Church the servants it needed. He it is who today gives us this new pastor. In thankfulness and joy we praise you, Lord.
The officiating pastor and his assistant(s) lay hands on the candidate.
We pray you, almighty Father, send your Holy Spirit on our brother N... N... whom we consecrate to your service and ordain pastor in your holy Church, minister of the Word and the sacraments.
The laying on of hands being thus completed, the officiant continues:
(there follows a series of petitions for the exercise of the ministry)'.[18]

This ordination rite shows clearly that it is Christ, dead, risen and glorified, who by the Holy Spirit, always gives the Church its pastors down the ages in the succession of the apostles, evangelists and witnesses created in the beginning. By laying his hands on the new pastor given by Christ to the Church, the officiant calls down the Holy Spirit upon him, consecrates him to God's service and ordains him pastor in the holy universal Church a minister of the word and sacraments. We find here all the essential elements of the ordination of ministers in the Church as it has been practised throughout Christian tradition.

In the light of that continued tradition we can present a summary of the doctrine as it appears on reading the New Testament:

1. *Choice by the Church*

The Holy Spirit is master of, as well as the criterion for, choice by the Church of candidates for ordination.

2. *Ministerial validation*

Ordination is performed on the responsibility of ministers of authority in the Church: in laying their hands on a candidate they are the instruments of the Holy Spirit and the representatives of the Church, which recognizes that God is sending it a new ambassador of his word, presence and authority.

3. *Sacramental epiclesis*

The act of ordination consists of prayer and the laying on of hands: it is
(a) an appeal to God for him to grant the power of the Holy Spirit,
(b) a sign of the Lord's answer in giving the spiritual gift of ministry,
(c) an offering to God of the new minister who is consecrated to his service.

4. *Apostolic mission*

The fruit of ordination is the gift of ministry, that is, the power of the Holy Spirit which sends men out on mission, in the name of Christ and the Church, and makes this mission effective to the glory of God.

Today, after the discussions of the Second Vatican Council and the Catholic liturgical reform conceptions of ordination to the ministry have come much closer together, even though there remain some important points to clarify, such as the nature or power of ministry, mission, or apostolic succession.[19]

Reformed tradition has been critical of the Catholic idea of the impression of an *indelible character* at ordination. On the one hand it is not doubted that the pastoral ministry has always been considered a ministry for life; but on the other hand there has been hesitation in accepting that ordination impressed an indelible character. The Discipline of the Reformed Churches of France of 1559 affirmed: 'Those elected once to the ministry of the word must understand that they are chosen to be ministers all their lives'.[20] The vows made by a pastor at his ordination today are prefaced thus: 'My brother, the service of God to which you are committing yourself is not one which can be taken or left according to interest or preference. Those who are called to the pastoral ministry must understand that they accept this charge for life, unless they are legitimately discharged for good and serious reasons'.[21] This last comment reveals the reason for Reformed criticism of the indelible character. It is a desire to keep the possibility of discharging someone from ministry for life for good and serious reasons. On this problem J.J. von Allmen writes:'But if we ask: is a character impressed for ever on a minister at the time of ordination? the question is embarrassing. If there is an unqualified "no" we may wonder whether we still hold firm to the unanimous conviction that a minister takes the place of Christ himself; but if there is an unqualified "yes" we may wonder what becomes of the right of the Church to depose ministers whose faith or way of life gives rise to scandal: can they still be stripped of their ministry if ordination has impressed an indelible character on them?'[22]

It must be remembered here that the Roman Catholic Church, while preserving the doctrine of the indelible character conferred by ordination, accepts the reduction to lay status of priests who for good and serious reasons cannot remain in the priesthood. So there must be some misunderstanding or evolution concerning this idea of the indelible character. It seems that either in certain Catholic treatises or in certain Protestant critiques there has been an idea of the priestly character which is too materialist or 'concretist'; hence the misunderstanding. A deeper biblical understanding of the doctrine of ordination and ministry on both sides brings new enlightenment; hence evolution.

Calvin's criticism of the indelible character reveals the poor teaching of his time and, consequently, a misunderstanding on his part:

'It is, if you please, the sacred oil which impresses an indelible character... But that character is spiritual. What has oil to do with the soul? Have they forgotten what they quote from Augustine, that if the word be withdrawn from the water, there will be nothing but water, but that it is owing to the word that it is a sacrament. What word can they show in their oil? Is it because Moses was commanded to anoint the sons of Aaron (Exod. 30.30)? ... They are attempting, forsooth, an ingenious device; they are trying, by a kind of patchwork, to make one religion out of Christianity, Judaism and Paganism'.[23] Here Calvin is criticizing a doctrine of the indelible character bound to a conception of anointing to the priesthood which is more inspired by the Old Testament than by apostolic practice. In his view this conception does not have the support of the word of God. However, he does not reject the idea of a 'spiritual character' any more than he is opposed to the sacramental nature of the laying on of hands, a 'sign of the spiritual grace of God'. What he does not accept is concretism with respect to the indelible character, underlined, in his view, by priestly anointing. There seems to have been much confusion in sixteenth-century Catholic theology over ordination rites; that would explain the strong reaction of Calvin, for whom the laying on of hands alone is the necessary apostolic action. That has now been clarified by the Catholic Church which regards the laying on of hands as the sacramental act of ordination and keeps anointing only as an explanatory rite. The conception of St Thomas Aquinas is, happily, abandoned. For the laying on of hands was part of preparing to receive the order, along with episcopal benediction and anointing which consecrated the ordinands, so that they might touch the sacrament. 'The conferring of power', writes St Thomas, 'is effected by giving them something pertaining to their proper act. And since the principal act of a priest is to consecrate the body and blood of Christ, the priestly character is imprinted at the very giving of the chalice under the prescribed form of words'.[24] This was a far cry from apostolic tradition.

Now that the grounds for dialogue between Catholics and Protestants have been completely renewed by a deeper biblical, patristic and liturgical understanding, is it possible to arrive at an ecumenical idea of the indelible character or of the power of order, to use the classic expressions of the school? Calvin said the character is spiritual. St Thomas defined it thus: 'The character of Order is a spiritual power... Every character is indelible. Therefore a character places a man in a state whence he cannot withdraw... For all that a man may return to the laity, the character always remains in him. This is evident from the fact that if he return to the clerical state, he does not receive again the Order which he had already'.[25]

We should remove from these terms 'character' and 'power' everything that could make them appear concrete, a mark or fluid. They must be understood in the light of the biblical word *exousia* which occurs so often in the New Testament and which means both 'power' and 'freedom' (*potestas, licentia*). The power a man receives depends on the freedom God grants him to exercise it. A passage from the Gospel illustrates well the significance of this term. It is the story of the healing of a paralytic where Jesus, in order to reveal his power to forgive sins, performed a miracle. For the Jews, only God could forgive sins; the revolution of Christ, which scandalized the Scribes, was that now God was giving this freedom or power to the Son of man and to the men who were to follow him in the faith: 'But that you may know that the Son of man has *authority (exousia) on earth to forgive sins"* — he then said to the paralytic — "Rise take up your bed and go home". And he rose and went home. When the crowds saw it, they were afraid, and they glorified God, who had given *such authority (exousia) to men*' (Matt. 9.6–8). We have seen, moreover, that the laying on of hands, together with the epicletic prayer, confers the gift of the Spirit for ministry, that is the power of the Holy Spirit which sends out on mission and gives love, understanding and strength for it to be carried out. After the laying on of hands Stephen was 'full of grace and power' (*dunamis*); through the laying on of hands Timothy received the spiritual gift of God: God gave him the 'spirit of power (*dunamis*), love and self-control' (Acts 6.8; 2 Tim. 1.6–7).

So, in the light of the New Testament, one can establish an equivalence between the spiritual gift of God (*charisma*), the power of the Spirit (*dunamis*) and the power or freedom given by God to perform a spiritual ministry (*exousia*). It is this gift of the Spirit, of power or authority, which constitutes the ministerial character, the distinctive sign of the minister ordained by the laying on of hands. St Thomas said: 'A character is a distinctive sign (*signum distinctivum*) ... The character of order (ministry) is a spiritual power'.[26] These definitions are acceptable so long as they are understood not in a static, concretist sense, but in the dynamic, biblical sense of *charisma*, *exousia* or *dunamis*. The spiritual power which constitutes the distinctive sign of the minister in the Church, his ministerial character, is not something at his disposal, a material mark, an injected fluid, a static treasure. It is a particular relation established by God with a believer whom he has chosen and ordained to be his ambassador within the universal priesthood of the Church. The ministerial character is a gift, but it remains a constant dialogue with God, a promise of renewal and revitalizing for the service of the Church and of men.[27] It is a spiritual power which is essentially a service of the unique power of God. It is a gift of *God* (2 Tim. 1.6), the authority of the *Son of God* (Matt. 9.6–8), the power of the *Spirit* (Acts 1.8). This gift of ministry can neither be separated nor made autonomous; it remains for ever bound to its creator, God, who grants from day to day, to him whom he has ordained, the freedom to exercise this spiritual authority in the name of Christ and in the power of the Spirit. Admittedly it is a *gift* of the Holy Spirit granted by the sacrament of the laying on of hands, but this gift is the establishing of a specific *relationship* between God and the minister, in which is constantly renewed, enlivened and enriched the spiritual authority of the Son of man exercised in his name by the man who is ordained. So the ministerial character is this specific relationship between God and his minister, created by ordination, this particular dialogue between Christ and his ambassador, inaugurated by the laying on of hands, this special communication between the Holy Spirit and his messenger, established by the spiritual gift of ministry. This relationship, dialogue and communication remain continuous and living, and must constantly be revived, although they are solidly established between God and the ordained minister, by the sacrament of the laying on of hands. Paul wrote to Timothy: 'I remind you to rekindle the gift of God that is within you through the laying on of my hands' (2 Tim. 1.6).

We have seen that for the Reformed tradition, as for the whole Catholic tradition, the pastoral ministry of the word and sacraments is definitive and lifelong. The spiritual gift of ministry is given once and for all in the laying on of hands. The specific relationship between God and his minister, created by ordination, is based on God's faithfulness. 'The gifts and the call of God are irrevocable', wrote St Paul (Rom. 11.29). We cannot imagine the apostles seeing their ministry as limited in time. 'I have fought the good fight, I have finished the race, I have kept the faith' (2 Tim. 4.7). God is faithful, despite the possible faithlessness of his ministers. 'God does not regret his gifts or his call' (an alternative translation of Rom. 11.29) ... 'If we are faithless, he remains faithful — for he cannot deny himself' (2 Tim. 2.13). Christian tradition has been based wholly on keeping the pastoral ministry for life and talks of the definitive character given to the minister at ordination. The classic term 'indelible character' has a somewhat materialist, concretist sound and it must be preferable to talk about 'definitive character'. Once again, it is God's faithfulness, symbolized in ordination by the sacramental laying on of hands, which establishes this definitive character of ministry, maintains this irrevocable gift and gives life to this indestructible relationship between God and his minister.

This definitive character of the pastoral ministry of the word and sacraments does not rule out the possibility of temporary ministries in the Church. As we have seen, there could be a diaconal ministry of limited duration. This temporary diaconate would be the object not of an ordination but of a commissioning or installation, in the presence of the community. Only the permanent or monastic diaconate, which is definitive, would be the object of an ordination.

But again, the definitive character of the pastoral ordained ministry does not rule out either the possibility of a return to lay status if ministers are 'legitimately discharged for good and serious reasons', in the words of the French Protestant liturgy. The Catholic Church also allows 'the reduction to the lay state'. Out of respect for ordination and the definite character it communicates, because of the faithfulness of God whose gifts and call are irrevocable (Rom. 11.29), the action of relieving a minister of his charge must be 'legitimate', that is, approved by the authority of the Church and based on 'good and serious reasons'. We need not go on to examine these possible reasons, for they can be very varied and it is the

Church who is the judge. Moreover, it may be a question of a simple hiatus in the exercise of a pastoral function and if the minister takes it up again one day he will not have to be ordained again, for he always keeps the definitive character of his ministry. As St Thomas correctly observed: 'If a man returns to the lay state, the character remains for ever in him. The proof is that if he returns to the ministry he does not receive again the order he already has'.[28]

The fact of not re-ordaining a minister who takes up his function in the Church again is based on the faithfulness of God, who does not revoke the specific relationship established between himself and a man by the sacrificial laying on of hands. Just as a Christian is not re-baptized after a period of indifference or renunciation of the faith, so a minister is not re-ordained after his ministry has been interrupted. Like the baptismal character, the ministerial character is definitive, for it is a spiritual gift from God who remains faithful even if we are faithless, for he cannot deny himself (2 Tim. 2.13).

The Protestant theologian J.-L. Leuba has clearly expressed this definitive character of the pastoral ministry in relation to God's faithfulness to his word: 'The Word has been spoken, in words and deeds, and the event of the Word has not happened... So be it! It is not ruled out in as much as it may happen again. At the Lord's Word the apostolic ministers will be able to continue casting their nets, even after having caught nothing, even after their preaching, witness and martyrdom have perhaps fallen on deaf ears and been displayed to unseeing eyes. Here to the highest degree the indelible character of ministry bursts forth. Nothing or no-one can erase the character by virtue of which God's possession of a man to make him a minister of his Word institutes a state such that the lack of anything happening could reduce to nothing. A state which, despite man's rebellion and that of its bearers themselves keeps flying the flag of promise, the instrument of the Holy Spirit, an instrument which remains an instrument even when for unfathomable reasons, arising from the mysteries of predestination, it is not used by the Holy Spirit'.[29]

13

THE APOSTOLIC MISSION
AND SUCCESSION

The pastoral vocation which God gives to a man cannot be recognized by the whole community. From the beginnings of the Church we see that the apostles, their helpers or successors are the instruments of the Holy Spirit, to discern vocations, and the organs of the Church, to give new ministers their mission. Paul wrote to Titus: 'This is why I left you in Crete, that you might amend what was defective, and appoint elders in every town as I directed you' (Titus 1.5). Each time that it is a question of ordination by the laying on of hands, this is performed by apostles or ministers who already have a function in the Church, like the prophets and teachers of the Church at Antioch (Acts 13.1–3). This type of ministerial succession has been a constant in the whole Christian tradition.

Calvin is very clear on this point: 'Lastly, it is to be observed, that it was not the whole people, but only pastors, who laid hands on ministers, though it is uncertain whether or not several always laid their hands'.[30] The whole of Reformed tradition is unanimous on this point. Only pastors may ordain other pastors and this not in a personal capacity but in a collegiate function, insofar as they constitute a presbytery, a presbyteral college, a pastoral body which is appointing for itself a new member. The reason is that one can only give what one has: only someone who has a pastoral ministry can hand it on.[31] Pastoral ministry being a gift and a mission from God, and not delegated from the community, it is not just any members of the community who perform ordination, but only those who have previously received this gift and mission. Then they act as instruments and signs of the Holy Spirit who transmits the spiritual gift of ministry. If they are delegated by the Church to perform the ordination of a new pastor, it is not in the sense that they might represent the community which is choosing itself new leaders, but in the sense that the community is asking them to carry out the pastoral ministry they have received to seek out and ordain a new minister. This transcendental dimension of ordination has always been present in the Reformed conception of the ministry.

But if, in principle, all pastors can ordain new pastors, in practice Reformed tradition has observed rules aimed at showing the ecclesial, ecumenical and catholic nature of the ministry. There are three possible rules: (1) the laying on of hands is performed by several pastors, at least three, or seven, or all those present; (2) one pastor ordains but he is chosen each time by a pastoral body who delegates him; (3) ordination is performed by a pastor whose function includes the duty of ordaining new pastors: the doyen, *antistes*, superintendent or bishop.[32] In each case the pastor or pastors who ordain are not acting personally but in the name of the Church or collegiately.[33] Although the title given to the pastor who ordains varies from one country to another, there is no deliberate intention to break with the ancient Catholic tradition whereby it is the bishop who performs ordination by the laying on of hands. But in as much as the Reformed Churches had been deprived of the ministry of bishops, they had in some way 'lowered' the episcopal ministry of ordination to the level of pastors, who could perform it either collegiately or by delegation of authority, or by a special function implying this duty. It was not forgotten that Western tradition had known, exceptionally, ordination by ministers other than bishops.

History indeed reveals cases of ordination by ministers who were not bishops. The Council of Ankara (314) states : 'Country bishops may not ordain presbyters or deacons, nor may town presbyters, unless permission is given in writing by the bishop, for each parish'.[34] Cassian quotes the case of an abbot who was a priest and had ordained priests and deacons.[35] In the eighth century we find the case of Willehad who formed Churches and ordained priests for them, without being a bishop.[36] In 1400 Boniface IX authorized the

Augustinian abbot of St Osith in the diocese of London to confer all orders, even the presbyterate.[37] In 1427 Martin V granted the same power, for five years, to the Cistercian abbot of Altzelle, in the diocese of Meissen.[38] So in exceptional cases it has been readily recognized that the presbyterate includes the possibility of ordination, even if it is only normally exercised, according to the discipline of the Church, by bishops. There are particular emergency cases where this possibility of using the presbyterate is activated by the delegation of authority.[39] It is this possibility which the Reformed Churches have exploited when they have not had the ministry of traditional bishops.[40]

So Reformed tradition, far from rejecting the episcopal ministry and the apostolic succession of its pastors, has been obliged, by force of circumstance, to remove them from their sociological and historical context, in order to maintain the theological justification of its church history. This was supported by the equivalence of the episcopal and presbyteral ministries in the apostolic Church and the possibility of ordination being performed by presbyters. A report presented to the General Assembly of the Church of Scotland in 1911 sums up well this traditional Reformed conception of the ministry of ordination. 'The Christian ministry is not derived from the people but from the pastors; a scriptual ordinance provides for this ministry being renewed by the ordination of a presbyter by presbyters; this ordinance originates with the apostles, who were themselves presbyters, and through them it goes back to Christ its source'.[41] Presbyteral or pastoral succession is the equivalent, in Reformed tradition, of episcopal succession: it is the apostolic succession of the ministry. One cannot underestimate the importance given to this ministerial apostolic succession.[42] However it does not in itself guarantee the continuity and faithfulness of the Church. A purely historical or mechanical succession of ministers, bishops or pastors would not mean *ipso facto* true apostolic succession in the Church. Ministerial succession by the laying on of hands should be the visible sign of a wider and deeper apostolic succession of the whole Church. Reformed tradition, following authentic Catholic tradition in this, distinguishes four realities which make up the true apostolic succession of the Church, symbolized, but not absolutely guaranteed, by ministerial succession. This doctrine of succession is expressed as follows:

'First, a true ministerial succession is organically related to *succession in doctrine*, that is in doctrinal obedience to the true teaching of the apostles...

Second, a true ministerial succession is organically related to the *Word which is ministered*...

Third, a true ministerial succession is organically related to the whole continuity of the redeemed life of the people of God. In other words, ministerial succession has its place only within *the basic continuity of the Church as the Body of Christ* on earth and in history. Here the focus of attention is to be directed to *Holy Baptism* as the sacrament of incorporation into Christ, and as the sacrament setting forth the fundamental union and communion of every member of the Body of Christ...

Fourth, a true ministerial succession is organically related to the continuous fellowship in the mystery of Christ which He freely grants in His grace. Here the focus of attention is upon the *Lord's Supper* as the sacrament in which we are ever granted renewal in the New Covenant of the Body and Blood of Christ...'[43]

So this résumé of the fundamental elements of true apostolic succession shows us that ministerial continuity without one of these elements would be deficient, but, conversely, these fundamental elements without the ministerial succession of the laying on of hands could not ensure true continuity, since this would be contrary to the rules of an apostolic order. 'The real and whole continuity of the Church through history in Christ, ministerial succession, or succession in the laying on of hands, is the episcopally appointed sign and attestation. Ministerial succession in no way secures the possession of the Holy Spirit nor does it guarantee a lawful ministry. But because it is the apostolically appointed ordinance, it cannot be condemned or neglected without disobedience and loss.[44]

So genuine apostolic succession consists of a composite faithfulness comprising: perseverance in the apostolic doctrine, the will to proclaim God's word, communion in the fundamental continuity of the Church, the Body of Christ, the faithful celebration of baptism and the Eucharist, and the succession in the laying on of hands, the sign of ministerial continuity. Pastoral or episcopal succession must be made to coincide with doctrinal apostolic succession to ensure the true continuity of the Church, which explains why the sixteenth-century Reformers did not hesitate to continue the life of the Church, despite the lack of bishops, using the means available. Without bishops they recognize presbyteral ministerial succession or they appealed to a prophetic ministry whose apostolic legitimacy was altered by its fruits.

'But these extraordinary ministers did not place the Church in the realm of the extraordinary. They did not start the Church all over again. They made it ordinary again by restoring the normal congruence between doctrinal and pastoral apostolic succession'.[45] So the sixteenth-century Reformation was carried out in the same genuine, total apostolic succession and not in the opposition to episcopal succession. Unfortunately the sin of men, on both sides, introduced a spirit of rapture into the intention of renewal, and that is why the Church's apostolic succession, instead of being solely enriched by doctrinal fullness and pastoral rediscovery, was dispersed in different currents. But it is for our age to rediscover this fullness of apostolic succession in the complementarity of obedience and faithfulness.[46]

There remains the major difficulty of reconciling Catholic and Protestant ideas of ministerial succession. Admittedly the Second Vatican Council has again brought out the doctrinal and sacramental aspects of the apostolic succession, in a way which to a certain extent matches the demands of the sixteenth-century Reformation. Yet, as far as true ministerial succession is concerned, no progress has been made in recognizing a valid ministry without ordination by a bishop who stands in historic succession.[47]

It is no doubt right that the Churches which were born of the Reformation and do not have episcopal ministry as the Catholic Church understands it, should ask themselves whether they should be re-establishing it in the light of the doctrinal developments of the Second Vatican Council. Indeed, if it was extraordinary circumstances which entailed the recognition of extraordinary paths for ministerial succession, why, without denying the validity of a prophetic ministry and a presbyteral succession, could one not go back to the general tradition of the Church before the Reformation, of a succession of the laying on of hands ensured by bishops, to signify doctrinal, sacramental and pastoral apostolic succession? Despite the psychological difficulties that this revival of a traditional episcopate might encounter among Protestants, there do not seem to be any insurmountable theological difficulties to stop it, at least so long as it is episcopacy in the sense of the early apostolic tradition as we have described it.

There are, on the other hand, much greater difficulties for Catholic theology, if it means recognizing the validity, however provisional, of a presbyteral ministerial succession. According to Catholic theology there has been a break in ministerial succession in Protestantism, since there has been a break in historical episcopal succession. Today, however, ecumenical dialogue, better knowledge of each other and the consideration of spiritual fruits produced outside the Catholic Church demand a fresh look at this radically divided position.[48] Such an examination is necessitated by the very logic of Catholic sacramentalism. If so many spiritual fruits ban be borne outside the apostolic succession, how to defend the need for the latter? If non-Catholic ecclesial communities are living without any real ministry and therefore any true Eucharist, and are bearing the fruits of the Spirit, are priesthood and the Eucharist really necessary? It is not enough to say that the Protestant Lord's Supper is a sacramental, while the Catholic Eucharist alone is a sacrament. We are brought back to the words of the Second Vatican Council, whose theological consequences must be fully acknowledged: 'We believe that especially because of the lack (*defectus*) of the Sacrament of Orders [the ecclesial Communities separated from us] have not preserved the genuine and total reality of the Eucharistic mystery' (p. 364). They have therefore preserved something of that reality: the commemoration of the Lord's death and resurrection, communion with Christ and the awaiting of His coming in glory, to use the words of the Council.[49] Is there then a real lack of the sacrament of orders, in an absolute, objective sense, or is it simply a lack of the complete sacrament in the sense given it by the Catholic Church? Is it not instead a weakness, inadequacy or fault in the sacrament of ordination? It is perhaps in a more refined interpretation of the expression of the Second Vatican Council, *praesertim propter Sacramenti Ordinis defectum*, and that there lies the hope of the ecumenical reply to the Catholic question concerning the ministry of the Reformed Churches.[50] Is the *defectus* mentioned absence or inadequacy?

Admittedly the official translation talks of the 'lack of the sacrament of orders', but the use of the word *defectus* elsewhere in the Decree on Ecumenism invites a less radical interpretation. Thus in the third paragraph the Council states: 'These separated Churches and Communities, though we believe they suffer from defects (*defectus*) already mentioned, have by no means been deprived of significance and importance in the mystery of salvation' (p. 346). Here it is obvious that the *defectus* is a weakness or inadequacy, not absence. And so the Council continues thus: 'The Spirit of Christ has not refrained from using them as means of salvation which derive their efficacy from the very fullness of grace and truth entrusted to the Catholic Church'.[52]

So it appears that the Council did not want all value to be denied to the ministry of the separated Churches, but wished to underline that because of a deficiency in ministry, these Churches 'have not preserved the genuine and total reality of the Eucharistic mystery'.

The Reformed Churches today know for certain that their ministry of the word and sacraments has borne the fruits of the Spirit, in a presbyteral and collegiate succession; so they could not accept that their pastors be denied their ministerial character: it would be for them offensive to Christ who called and ordained them to the service of God's people. The Reformed Churches must certainly rediscover the traditional episcopate in the interests of the visible unity of Christians, but it can only be achieved with respect for the ministry they already have; basically it is a question of finding the convergence of presbyteral and episcopal succession, recognizing and respecting what Christ the sovereign priest has worked in each, through the word and the sacraments, making good, where necessary, their accidental deficiencies in the full apostolic succession, doctrinal, sacramental and pastoral.[53]

We find this idea of Christ making good the accidental deficiencies of ministry in a seventeenth-century Reformed theologian, obviously applied in an apologetic sense, in reply to Catholic accusations that the Reformed ministry was invalid. Jean Daillé makes these comments on the catechism:

'We are reproached with the fact that some of our Ancestors lacked the laying on of hands. But firstly, supposing but not granting that there was some shortcoming in the ordination of one of them, why should it be held against me as a crime? If there was such rigidness, there would be no Prelate in the Roman Church who could be sure of being right... Next I deny that our predecessors lacked the order. Who knows what it was for most of the Priests or Bishops, including even people holding office in the Roman Communion. That if one of them lacked this character the fault was repaired by the confirmation of others who associated themselves with him and recognized him as brother, as we know that often the non-validity of the ordination of a prelate was covered in the early Church, by the approval and consent of the other prelates. Finally, consecration by the hand of another pastor must still be held to be truly necessary, whenever and wherever possible, but if not the vocation does not cease to be valid without it, provided the other parts are there, that is the people's wish and approval and the ability and consent of the one who is called, as, for example, if a ship had run aground on some heathen shore, bringing there many Christians who had neither a Pastor nor any means of having one come from elsewhere. Who can doubt that in this case, if there was someone among them who had the gifts and the inclination, could he not with a clear conscience carry out this duty, being called to it by the wish and common consent of the whole flock? Necessity excuses the lack of formalities, and where this happens it must be considered certain that it is God who is calling us. Now Christianity was reduced to a similar necessity in the time of our Fathers...'[54]

This passage is interesting and revealing from several points of view. In a preceding paragraph Daillé first stated that what was supremely important was that the Church should have ministries which conformed to the order of Christ and the apostles: 'Our opponents say that we have no vocation; they would be right if we had established charges that neither Jesus Christ nor his disciples had laid down...'

Thus Daillé's thought, which is typical of Reformed theology, develops in four stages which we shall summarize here, for they seem to us very useful in ecumenical research.

(a) *The apostolic doctrine of ministries* is as important to the

Church as the apostolic succession of the laying on of hands. Indeed, what would be the use of a ministerial succession which established ministers that neither Christ nor the apostles had instituted?

(b) *The presbyteral or episcopal origin* of the ministry in the Churches born of the Reformation creates a true apostolic succession in the laying on of hands; the fact that the first Reformed ministers had been priests or bishops of the Roman Catholic Church is not irrelevant, for it ensures the pastoral, presbyteral or episcopal succession of ordination in the Reformed Churches.

(c) *Supplementation by the Church*, done with the approval and consent of the ordained ministers, has made good the possible accidental and unknowing lack of ordination in certain of its pastors; in fact the confirmation of a ministry *de facto* by its integration into the pastoral body makes up for a 'shortcoming in ordination'.

(d) *The extraordinary ministry* can be raised up by God in cases of extreme necessity, where neither ministerial succession by the laying on of hands nor the confirmation of a minister by receiving him into the pastoral body can be ensured; in such cases the extraordinary minister is validated by 'the desire and approval of the people, the ability and consent of the one who is called', but this extraordinary ministry can only have a single, provisional function with the aim of reestablishing an ordinary ministry, for 'consecration by the hand of another pastor is in truth necessary, when and where it is available'.

Obviously these cases of supplementation and extraordinary ministry are understood in different ways by Catholic and Protestant theologians. The latter only consider them in exceptional circumstances where pastoral succession by the laying on of hands, by presbyters or bishops, is lacking; Catholic theologians would resort to them in all cases of the ministry of the Reformed Churches, since they cannot accept the validity of pastoral succession outside the historical community of the Catholic Church such as they understand it. However, common research in this direction, with a view to the mutual recognition of ministries, seems to us very promising, the beginning of a genuine restoration of visible, organic unity between the Churches.[55]

CONCLUSION

CONCLUSION

The argument concerning ministry today may be seen as having three major themes: dislike of clerical separation, criticism of the institutional parish and accusations of hierarchical authority. The solution to this dispute will only be found in rediscovering the identity and specific nature of ministry; it will depend on the answer to this question: what is a pastor within the priestly people of the Church? We have tried to find an answer in this book by removing from revealed truth and sound tradition all that history has added as an unnecessary burden to ministry in the Church.

Today some priests or pastors find it difficult to cope with the feeling of being apart from the everyday life of men, separated from the world by a clerical existence. There is no doubt that, especially since the sixteenth century, ministers of the Church have become people of distinction, clerks and intellectuals, who are separate from others. This was tolerable in a society where religion was built in as an essential structure. For some it could even be social promotion to become priests or pastors. With the secularization of modern Western society the Christian minister can no longer find his social role among men. That is in one sense a healthy purifying of the ministry. In fact, the minister, stripped of all his sociological privileges, is seen more clearly in his fundamental nature of an ambassador for Jesus Christ, the prophet who was rejected and crucified but victorious in the power of the Spirit.

To be fully man and modern, the pastor seeks to be better integrated into the society of which he feels a part. He no longer wants to be an official in worship, but one who has been sent by, and is a sign of, Christ in the priestly people of Christians. Just as a father is not paid to carry out his work in his family, so the pastor would like to earn his living like everyone else, so as not to receive a salary as a leader in the Christian community. But would it be possible for him to carry out his ministry alongside his job? Admittedly there will always be a need for full-time pastors, but it is quite valid to allow ministers of the Church the freedom to work if they wish, perhaps, moreover, just for a while. That would require a greater number of pastors, speedier, more basic training, and ordination spread more widely among God's people.

For the Catholic Church in the West there is a problem of the celibacy of priests. Some are in rather too much hurry to abandon this value which has so greatly increased the force of the ministry in the history of the Roman Church. Before new decisions are taken, ecumenical dialogue must instruct priests on the difficulty of uniting ministry and family responsibilities. It seems that the obvious way to restore the free choice of celibacy as vocation and spiritual gift must be the ordination to the presbyterate of married men who have shown their worth in family responsibility, 'for if a man does not know how to manage his own household, how can he care for God's Church?' (1 Tim. 3.5).

As we have seen, the Church of the future will have to be very liberal in its attitudes to forms of communities which grow up locally. The parish solution is not the only one. The orientation must be much more towards small life-size communities, ready to be regrouped in bigger units on certain occasions. That, moreover, fits in with the view of an increasing number of wage-earning pastors and a large number of laity doing diaconal work, if only temporarily.

Today's argument also concerns the exercise of authority in the Church. The ecclesiological developments of the Second Vatican Council have given the bishop a great deal of power. Some developments in collegiality could turn the episcopal order into a sort of supreme ecclesiastic caste, from which would flow all power and functions in the Church. To avoid this deviation, collegiality between bishops and presbyters must be developed. The rediscovery of a theology of the episcopate at the Second Vatican Council must be completed by the concrete, living realization of the collegiality of presbyters gathered round the bishop. For this idea to be feasible, perhaps the number of bishops would also have to be increased? The solution to the problem of authority in the Church lies in collegiality and solidarity among bishops, presbyters and deacons, in the service of a single ministry which takes different forms within the priestly people of God.

And this unique ministry, increased and diversified, will always remain the ambassadorship of reconciliation in the name of Christ, by means of God's word and sacraments of his presence, in the power of the Spirit which brings men together in the unity of the Church, the sign of the love of Christ crucified and risen again.

NOTES

PART ONE
THE PRIESTHOOD OF CHRIST

1. C. Spicq, *L'Epitre aux Hébreux*, Gabalda, Paris, 1952–53; cf. especially vol. II, pp. 249–259.
2. This theme of the one true priest has been widely developed by the Church Fathers: Clement of Alexandria, *Stromateis* II, V; Origen, *Homilies on Joshua* 16, 2; Eusebius of Caesarea, *Demonstratio Evangelica*, IV, 10, 16; Cyril of Jerusalem, *Catechism* XI, 1; St. Jerome, *Letters* 22, 23, and St. Ambrose, *De officiis* 1, 48, follow the same doctrine.
3. Tertullian, *Against Marcion*, saw Christ as *authenticus pontifex Dei Patris* (4, 35) and *proprius et legitimus Dei antistes* (5, 9), the one high priest and bishop.
4. See J. Lécuyer, *Le sacerdoce dans le mystère du Christ*, Le Cerf, Paris, 1957, pp. 9–20 (chapter 1: 'L'unique vrai prêtre').
5. On this subject see the fine exposition by Calvin, *Institutes of the Christian Religion* II, XII, 1.
6. K. Barth, *Church Dogmatics* vol. IV part 1, para. 58, 2: 'The being of a Man in Jesus Christ'. Theses pages by Barth on substitution and reconciliation contain some of the most powerful writing of the Christian tradition. (English Edition, Edinburgh, 1956, pp. 92–122).
7. Some Eastern Fathers have insisted on this ordination of Christ in the Jordan. For Theodorus Studios, Orat, 3, *In Vigil. luminum* 5 John the Baptist is 'the priest of Christ the high priest' to give Jesus his messianic priesthood. St Ephraim, *Commentary on the Diatessaron*, 4, expresses it thus: 'Christ received through John the Baptist the dignity of prophet and priest. He received by birth the royal dignity of the house of David, for he was born of the house of David; but he received the priesthood of the house of Levi at his second birth, at the baptism performed by a son of Aaron'.

8. Aphrahat of Syria, *De Persecutione*, 13, expressed thus Christ's ordination orientating him towards suffering: 'David was anointed by Samuel to be king instead of Saul who had sinned; and Jesus was anointed by John to be high priest instead of the priests, the ministers of the Law. David was persecuted after his anointing; and Jesus was persecuted after His anointing'. In *Nicene and post-Nicene Fathers of the Christian Church* (2nd Series) vol. XIII (Oxford-New York, 1898), p. 397.

9. C.H. Dodd, *The Interpretation of the Fourth Gospel*, Cambridge University Press, 1958, p. 401 ff; H. Strathmann, *Das Evangelium nach Johannes*, Vandenoeck und Ruprecht, Göttingen, 1953.

10. This doctrine of the three functions of Christ is a precept of tradition which Calvin was particularly careful to bring to light again; he devotes a whole chapter of the *Institutes* to it (II, XV: 'Three things chiefly to be regarded in Christ — viz. his offices of Prophet, King and Priest'), (Trans. by H. Beveridge, London, 1949).

11. K.H. Rengsdorf, *Das Evangelium nach Lukas*, Vandenhoeck und Ruprecht, Göttingen, 1952, p. 70.

12. P. Bonnard, *L'Evangile selon saint Matthieu*, Delachaux et Niestlé, Neuchâtel, 1963, p. 64.

13. Judaism knew this reconciliation in the context of the liturgy, but its aim was to avoid personal defilement and that of the Temple; each has to beware of 'not defiling his Holy Spirit' (*Ecrit de Damas*), VI, 14–VII, 4). Here Christ is not making reconciliation a condition of ritual purity but a fundamental element of the liturgy itself.

14. S. Lyonnet, 'La sotériologie paulinienne', *Introduction à la Bible*, II, pp. 874–77.

15. 'The sacrifice of Calvary was so perfect, because of the feelings of the victim who was offering himself, that God decided that it would be the supreme sacrifice. The infinite is unique. Henceforth material sacrifices were abolished and there would be one religion in spirit and in truth, for God himself is spirit'. C. Spicq, *Op.cit.*, p. 307.

16. The term *logikos* means 'that which concerns the deepest being, in contrast to the formal, the external, the appearance. So the expression would emphasize that the sacrifice of the 'body-person' fully commits the whole being, perhaps in opposition to the ancient sacrifices who placed on the altars the bodies of animals', F.-J. Leenhardt, *L'Epître de saint Paul aux Romains*, Delachaux et Niestlé, Neuchâtel, 1957, pp. 170–71.

17. J. Colson, *Ministre de Jésus-Christ ou le sacerdoce de l'Evangile*, Beauchesne, Paris, 1966, pp. 99–109.

18. Among the various lists of ministries of the old covenant (Mic. 3.11; Ezek. 7.26..) which give particular importance to the triad: heads, priests, prophets, that of Jeremiah (2.8) identifies the king and shepherd. Cf. S. Amsler, 'Les ministères de l'ancienne alliance: rois, prêtres et prophètes'. *Ministères et laïcat*, Presses de Taizé, 1964, pp. 29–41.

19. On the identicalness of the Messiah-King, the paschal lamb and the suffering servant, see F.-M. Braun, *Jean le théologien*, II, Gabalda, Paris, 1964, pp. 69–86.

20. F.-M. Braun, *Op.cit.*, pp. 99–101.

21. This doctrine of the sharing of the Church's ministry in that of Christ, prophet, priest and King, crucified and risen, has been clearly expressed by the Second Vatican Council: 'When Jesus rose up again after suffering death on the cross for mankind, He manifested that He had been appointed Lord, Messiah and Priest forever (cf. Acts 2.36; Heb. 5.6; 7.17–21), and He poured out on His disciples the Spirit promised by the Father (cf. Acts 2.33)' [*Lumen Gentium* 5]. 'By sacred ordination and by the mission they receive from their bishops, priests are promoted to the service of Christ, the Teacher, the Priest and the King. They share in His ministry of unceasingly building up the Church on earth into the People of God, the Body of Christ and the Temple of the Holy Spirit' [*Presbyterorum Ordinis* 1].

PART TWO
THE APOSTOLIC MINISTRY

1. K.H. Rengsdorf, 'Apostolos', *Theologisches Wörterbuch zum Neuen Testament* I, G. Kittel, Stuttgart, 1933, pp. 406–408. If the twelve were instituted by Christ, the name 'apostle' probably comes later. The Christian community chose it because they are characterized by Christ's mission (*apostellein*: to send out); E.M. Kredel, 'Der Apostelbegriff in der neuesten Exegese', *Zeitschrift für katholische Theologie* 78, 1956, pp. 169–93, 257–305; X. Léon-Dufour, 'Apôtres', *Vocabulaire de théologie biblique*, Le cerf, Paris, 1964, pp. 54–59; G. Klein, *Der Ursprung des Zwölfapostolats*, Göttingen, 1961; B. Rigaux, 'Les douze apôtres', *Concilium* 34, 1968, pp. 11–18; D. Müller, 'Apostel', *Bibeltheologisches Wörterbuch* 1, 1968, pp. 31–38.

2. F. Büchsel, 'Deo (luo)', *ThWbNT* II, G. Kittel, Stuttgart, 1935, pp. 59–60; P. Bonnard, *Op.cit.*, p. 275.

186

3. O. Cullmann, *Saint-Pierre*, Delachaux et Niestlé, Neuchâtel, 1952, p. 201 ff.
4. G. Martelet, 'Eléments transmissibles et intransmissibles de la succession apostolique', *Verbum Caro* 58, 1961, pp. 185–98.
5. J. Schmitt, 'Sacerdoce juif et hiérarchie', *Revue des sciences religieuses*, 1935, pp. 257–58.
6. This election of Matthias appears to be a Christianized variant of an old Jewish ritual of election to the function of *paqid* or *mabaqqer*, a ritual where, moreover, the three typical elements are found: Scripture, *pesher* (commentary), prayer. J. Colson, 'La succession apostolique au niveau du premier siècle', *Verbum Caro* 58, 1961, pp. 144–46.
7. J.-L. Leuba, *L'insitution et l'événement*, Delachaux et Niestlé, Neuchâtel.
8. G. Dix, 'The Ministry in the early Church', in *The Apostolic Ministry*, Hodder and Stoughton, London, 1964, pp. 230–31.
9. J. Colson, *Les fonction ecclésiales*, Desclée de Brouwer, Paris, 1956, pp. 73–91.
10. A.M. Farrer, 'The Ministry in the New Testament', in *The Apostolic Ministry*, Hodder and Stoughton, London, 1964, pp. 133–42. A.M. Farrer relates the mission of the seventy on the one hand to that of the seventy elders in the time of Moses, and on the other to the institution of the seven in the Church at Jerusalem; St Luke is then trying to justify the presbyteral ministry alongside the apostolate.
11. R. Paquier, 'L'épiscopate dans la structure institutionnelle de l'Eglise', *Verbum Caro* 49, 1959, p. 32.
12. 'The sequence of events presents an undeniable parallelism:

Bright cloud covers the tabernacle.	Bright cloud of Christ's transfiguration.
Solemn departure of the people for the promised land.	Solemn departure of the Messiah for Jerusalem.
God's fire falls on those who protest.	The fire of heaven called upon the Samaritans by the apostles.
Institution of the seventy elders to assist Moses.	Choice and sending out of the seventy by the Lord.'

R. Paquier, *Op.cit.*, p. 32; cf. A.M. Farrer, *Op.cit.* p. 137.
13. 'The supposition that the seven are regarded by St Luke as "deacons" is a very old error'. A.M. Farrer, *Op. cit.*, p. 138.
14. J. Colson, *Op. cit.*, pp. 113–24.
15. P. Benoît, *Exégèse et théologie* III, Le Cerf, Paris, 1961, p. 236. P. Benoît sees the ministry of bishops as a development of that of the presbyters because of the increasing number of communities: '... and these ministries would be called Bishops and Deacons, no doubt under the influence of the Greek-speaking setting...'
16. J. Guilko, *Der Philipperbrief*, Freiburg, 1968, pp. 32–40.

17. On the whole question of the origin of ministries from New Testament times see W. Michaelis, *Das Ältestament der christlichen Gemeinde im Lichte des heiligen Schrift*, Berne, 1953; E. Schweizer, *Gemeinde und Gemeindeordnung im Neuen Testament*, Zürich, 1959; H. von Campenhausen, 'Die Anfänge des Priesterbegriffes in der alten Kirche', *Tradition und Leben*, Tübingen, 1960, pp. 272–89; E. Käsemann, 'Amt und Gemeinde im Neuen Testament', *Exegetische Versuche und Besinnungen*, I, Göttingen, 1960, pp. 103–34; K.H. Schelkle, *Disciple et Apôtre*, Mappus, Lyon, 1965; G. Romaniuk, *Le sacerdoce dans le Nouveau Testament*, Mappus, Lyon, 1966.

18. C. Spicq, *Les Epîtres pastorales*, Gabalda, Paris, 1947; K.H. Schelkle, *Introduction au Nouveau Testament*, Mulhouse, 1965, pp. 217–26; P. Dornier, *Les Epîtres pastorales*, Gabalda, Paris, 1969.

19. C. Spicq, *Op. cit.*, pp. 125–34.

20. T.F. Torrance, *Conflict and Agreement in the Church*, II, Lutterworth Press, London, 1960, pp. 30–57; J.M. Barkley, 'La signification de l'ordination', *Verbum Caro* 43, 1957, pp. 226–50.

21. K.H. Schelkle, 'Services et serviteurs dans les Eglises au temps du Nouveau Testament', *Concilium* 43, 1969, pp. 11–22.

22. J. Dupont, *Le discours de Milet*, Le Cerf, Paris, 1962.

23. If, following numerous commentators, the 'angels' of the seven Churches of the Apocalypse (Revelation 2–3) must be seen as ministers representing and personifying them, then the seven letters of St. John reveal the existence of a personal episcopal ministry in the Church of Asia Minor at the end of the first century. This would be a new link in the chain of evolution. This interpretation of the angel-bishop is found in Strack-Billerbeck, Ewald, Weiss, Zahn, Hadorn, Knevels, Barth (*Church Dogmatics* III/3)....; cf. C. Brutsch, *Clarté de l'Apocalypse*, Labor et Fides, Geneva, 1955, p. 39; A. Feuillet *L'Apocalypse*, Desclée de Brouwer, Paris, 1962, p. 41.

24. Ignatius of Antioch, *Letters*, in Bishop Lightfoot, *The Apostolic Fathers*.

25. C. Dillenschneider, *Le Christ, l'unique prêtre*, Alsatia, Paris, 1960, pp 36–56.

26. It was a long time before the Church readopted this title for its ministers: Tertullian *Treaty on Baptism* XVIII, 1, once calls the bishop 'high priest' in connection with the minister of the sacrament: '*Dandi quidem summum habet ius summus sacerdos, si qui est, episcopus...*'; Hippolytus, *Against Heresies* I, 6 refers once to the function of the high priest of the apostles (*archiierateia*); Eusebius, *History of the Church* X, IV, 2, addresses ministers in these terms: 'Friends of God, priests

(*hiereis*) dressed in the holy garment'; cf. K.H. Schelkle, *Concilium*, 43, p. 12.

27. Calvin, *Catechism of the Church of Geneva*, in *Calvin's Tracts* vol. II (trans. Beveridge), Edinburgh, 1849, p. 83.

28. *Ibid.*, p. 93.

29. *La confession de foi des Eglises réformées de France* and *La confession de foi des Eglises réformées wallonnes et flamandes des Pays-Bas*, Je Sers, Paris, 1934, pp. 166–68 and 222–25.

30. *Ibid.*, p. 167 and 223–24.

31. J. Daillé, *Sermons sur le Catéchisme des Eglises réformées*, Geneva, 1701, III, pp. 645–46.

32. D. Chamier, *Panstratiae Catholicae*, Geneva, 1626, IV, 1 ch, 13, 3, p. 28; see B. Hubsch *Le ministère des prêtres et des pasteurs*, thèse dactylographiée, Faculté de théologie de Lyon, 1965.

PART THREE
EPISCOPATE, PRESBYTERATE AND DIACONATE

1. See for example: Mgr Guerry, *L'evêque*, Fayard, Paris, 1954; *L'épiscopat et l'Eglise universelle*, various authors, coll. *Unam Sanctam* 39, Le Cerf, Paris, 1962; *The Historic Episcopate*, various authors, Dacre Press, London, 1960; A.G. Herbert, *Apostle and Bishop*. Faber and Faber, London, 1963; G. Gassmann, *Das historische Bischofsamt und die Einheit der Kirche*, Vanderhoeck und Ruprecht, Göttingen, 1964; *Eglises chrétiennes et épiscopat*, various Catholic and Protestant authors, Mame, Paris, 1966.

2. Eusebius, *The History of the Church* (trans. Williamson), Penguin, 1965, p. 148.

3. 'Starting from the other end', J.A.T. Robinson, *The New Reformation?*, SCM Press, London, 1965.

4. There is some debate on the interpretation of 1 Tim. 4.14. Some think that it was not a laying on of hands 'by the presbytery' but laying hands 'on the presbyter', which would mean that Timothy was ordained to the presbyterate: D. Daube, *The New Testament and Rabbinic Judaism*, Oxford, 1956, pp. 244–46; J. Jeremias, *Zeitschrift für neutestamentliche Wissenschaft und die Kunde der älteren Kirche*, Berlin, 1957, vol. XLVIII, pp. 127–32; J. Dupont, *Le Discours de Milet*, Le Cerf, Paris, 1962, p. 140. It is curious to note that Calvin was already putting forward this interpretation: 'For what is said in the First Epistle of the *laying on of hands of the presbytery*, I do not

understand as if Paul were speaking of the College of Elders. By the expression I understand the ordination itself; as if he had said, Act so, that the gift which you received by the laying on of hands, when I made you a presbyter, may not be in vain' (*Institutes* IV, III, 16 — p. 326). This interpretation runs into difficulty because Timothy is nowhere called presbyter, not even in the Epistle addressed to him, which is at least surprising in these texts which attribute such importance to various ministries and their titles; furthermore, if Timothy received the laying on of hands at Lystra, as is generally thought (C. Spicq, *Op. cit.*, p. xxxiii), it is improbable that he should have been ordained to the presbyterate, a local and stable ministry, when he was chosen by Paul as his fellow worker for his missionary journeys. It is much more logical to suppose that it was the presbytery at Lystra (cf. Acts 14.23, 'they had appointed elders from them') led by Paul for the occasion, which laid hands on Timothy for his ministry as the apostle's fellow worker. There is no contradiction between 1 Tim. 4.14 and 2 Tim. 1.6 for in the first the apostle insists on prophecy, that is the witness of the Church (cf Acts 16.2: '(Timothy) was well spoken of by the brethren at Lystra and Iconium'), so it is a question of the presbytery; and in the second the apostle has in mind the personal relation binding him to Timothy so he underlines his role in the ordination (2 Tim. 1.6). Besides, it can be shown that the genitive *tou presbuteroi*, 'of the presbytery', is subjective and not absolute, by comparing it with 2 Tim. 1.6, 'through the laying on *of my* hands' or in Acts 8.18: 'through the laying on *of the apostles* ' hands'. So we prefer the current interpretation, defended again by G. Bornkamm, *ThWbNT*, VI, G. Kittel, Stuttgart, 1959, p. 666 n. 92. On the difference between 1 Tim. 4.14 and 2 Tim. 1.6 he draws attention to the fact that the nature of the two epistles is different: the first presents a rule of the community and it is normal that it should concern the ordination by the presbytery; the second is the apostle's testament, and it is understandable that he should recall his personal role in the ordination of his fellow worker and spiritual son.

5. *Institutes* IV, IV, 4.

6. Lohse, *Die Ordination im Spätjudentum und im Neuen Testament*, Vandenhoeck and Ruprecht, Göttingen, 1951.

7. '*De meo animo sic accipe: mihi si detur optio, quidvis libentius sim facturus, quam ut tibi hic optemperem; sed quoniam non esse mei juris memini, cor meum velut mactatum Domino in sacrificium offero*'. Calvin's seal shows a hand holding a heart offering it to God.

8. F.J. Leenhardt, *Op. cit.*, p. 207: 'Priesthood is henceforth

assumed by the apostolate not in as much as the priest would officiate at a new altar to offer a new sacrifice, but in that he announces the Gospel and becomes the instrument by which the Holy Spirit associates believers with the sacrifice of the cross'. K.H. Schelkle, *Disciple et apôtre*, Mappus, Lyon, 1965, pp. 106–19.

9. K. Weiss, 'Paulus Priester', *Theologische Literaturzeitung*, 1954.

10. The Book of Exodus, Ecumenical translation of the Bible, Les Bergers et les Mages, Le Cerf, Paris, 1969, p. 122.

11. A. Rose, *Psaumes et prière chrétienne*, Saint-André, Bruges, 1965; A.M. Roguet, *Le miel du rocher ou la douceur des psaumes*, Le Cerf, Paris, 1967.

12. *Prière du temps présent, le nouvel office divin*, Desclée de Brouwer, Desclée, Labergerie, Mame, Paris, 1969.

13. On the ecumenical nature of this doctrine, see Foi et Constitution, 'Accord oecuménique sur l'eucharistie', *Verbum Caro* no. 87, 1969, pp. 1–10.

14. Cf. our article 'La théologie des nouvelles prières eucharistiques', *La Maison-Dieu* no. 94, 1968, pp. 77–102.

15. *Institutes*, IV, XV.

16. Constitution *Lumen Gentium*, 29; Mgr Philips, *L'Eglise et son mystère*, I, Desclée Paris, 1967, pp. 374–90. Among the many works which have paved the way for restoring the diaconate, see K. Rahner, H. Vorgrimler, etc., *Diaconia in Christo, Uber die Erneuerung des Diakonats* (Quaest. Disp. 15/16) Freiburg in Br., 1962.

17. J. Colston, *La fonction diaconale aux origines de l'Eglise*, Desclée de Brouwer, Paris 1960.

18. *Letters* X, 96; Origen, Commentary on Romans X, 17, calls *ministrae* women who are 'instituted for ministry'.

19. *Apostolic Constitution* VIII, 19–20, 24.

20. J. Danielou, 'Le ministère des femmes dans l'Eglise ancienne', *La Maison-Dieu*, 61, 1960, pp. 70–96; A Kerkvoorde, *Où en est le problème du diaconat*, Apostolat liturgique, Bruges, 1961, pp. 36–45.

21. F. Méjan, *Disciple de l'Eglise réformée de France*, Je Sers, Paris, 1947, p. 303.

22. *Das Buch der Basler Reformation*, p. 201.

23. J.-J. von Allmen, *Le saint ministère*, Delachaux et Niestlé, Neuchâtel, 1968, p. 189.

24. It may seem surprising that in this book we are not touching on the problem of the ordination of women to the presbyterate, raised by some Protestant Churches. The reason is that this problem does not seem to us really theological or ecclesiological, but rather sociological and ecumenical. We would prefer the Churches to tackle this question together, to find a common

answer suited to modern society, rather than create new gulfs between each other by arriving at separate decisions. While waiting for this ecumenical problem to be properly solved the diaconal ministry of women could be developed in the very broad sense that we are suggesting. It would be the best way to approach sensibly the problem of the female pastorate; here again the female diaconate could play a bridging role, one of transition and probation. See the World Council of Churches, *On the Ordination of Women*, Geneva, 1964.

25. See also the *Motu proprio 'Sacrum diaconatus ordinem'* by Paul VI on the restoration of the permanent diaconate in the Roman Church, ch. V, no. 22, Le Centurion, Paris 1967, pp. 122–24.
26. The World Council of Churches, *The Ministry of Deacons*, Geneva, 1965; H. Denis, R. Schaller, *Diacres dans le monde d'aujourd'hui*, Apostolat des éditions, Lyon, 1967.
27. See the interesting suggestions by A. Kerkvoorde, *op. cit.*, 'Diaconat et vie religieuse', pp. 46–56.

PART FOUR
ORDINATION TO THE MINISTRY

1. On ordination by the presbytery see the discussion of 1 Tim. 4.14 in note 4 of Part III.
2. T.F. Torrance, *Conflict and Agreement in the Church*, 2, Lutterworth Press, London, 1960, pp. 30–46.
3. *The Apostolic Tradition of Hipploytus*, trans. by B.S. Easton, C.U.P. 1934, reprinted Archon Books, 1962, p. 230.
4. Ibid., pp. 34–35. We have tried to bring out the different elements in this prayer typographically, following the example of A. Rose, 'La prière de consécration pour l'ordination épiscopale', *Au service de la parole de dieu*, Mélanges offerts à Mgr. A.-M. Charue, Bishop of Namur, Duclot, Gembloux, pp. 129–45; he also draws on the version by B. Botte, *La Tradition apostolique de saint Hippolyte*, Essai de reconstitution, Münster 1963, pp. 7–11.
5. Apostolic Constitution, *Pontificalis Romani recognito*, Rome, 18 June 1968.
6. H. Denziger, *Ritus Orientalium*, Graz, 1961, pp. 23–24.
7. J. Lecuyer, 'La prière d'ordination de l'éveque', *Nouvelle Revue Théologique*, 6 (June 1967), p. 605.
8. There is an inevitable parallel between this phrase *offere dona sancta ecclesiae tuae* and that of the Eucharistic prayer that follows the ordination of the bishop, *petimus ut mittas spiritum*

tuum sanctum in oblationem sanctae ecclesiae (*Apostolic Tradition* 4); these expressions of offering 'belong originally to the vocabulary of spiritual worship in the New Testament and early Christian writing. But they gradually acquired Eucharistic usage' (A. Rose, Op. cit., p. 140); see J. Juglar, *Le sacrifice de louange*, (Lex Orandi) 15, Le Cerf, Paris, 1953, pp. 133–59.

9. *Apostolic Tradition*, p. 37.
10. Ibid., p. 39.
11. *Christian Institutes*, IV, III, 16.
12. Ibid, IV, XIV, 20.
13. Ibid., IV, XIX, 28.
14. Ibid., IV, XIV, 1.
15. Ibid., IV, XIX, 31. On this doctrine see L. Schummer, *Le ministère pastoral dans l'Institution chrétienne de Calvin à la lumière du troisième sacrement*, Franz Steiner Verlag, Wiesbaden, 1964, pp. 318–27. There should be noted here the development of Calvin's thought under the influence of Bucer during his stay at Strasbourg concerning the sacramentality of the laying on of hands; it can be seen in the various editions of the *Christian Institutes*. 'Bucer would have liked, one day, to introduce "sacrament" for confession, marriage and ordination'. J. Courvoisier, *La notion d'Eglise chez Bucer dans son développement historique*, Alcan, Paris, 1933, p. 127. At Strasbourg the laying on of hands was accompanied by this text: 'Receive the Holy Spirit, protector and support against all evil, strength and help for all good, from the merciful hand of God the Father, Son and Holy Spirit'.
16. J. Daillé, *Sermons*, on 2 Tim., p. 91.
17. B. Hubsch, 'Le ministère des prêtres et des pasteurs', *Verbum Caro*, 77, 1966, p. 39.
18. Eglise Réformée de France, *Liturgie*, Berger-Levrault, Paris, p. 260.
19. This coming together is particularly noticeable in the area of spirituality of the ministry; see, for example, K. Rahner, *Serviteurs du Christ*, Mame, Paris, 1969, 'Pour une rénovation d'ordination', pp. 275–82.
20. Article 12.
21. *Liturgie*, Op. cit., p. 259.
22. Op. cit., p. 53.
23. *Christian Institutes*, IV, XIX, 31.
24. St Thomas Aquinas, *Summa Theologica*, III (Supplement) QQ.XXXIV–LXVIII, Burn Oates & Washbourne Ltd., 1922, Quest. 37, art. 5.
25. Ibid., Quest. 35, art. 2.
26. Ibid., p. 13.
27. K. Rahner, Op. cit., p. 277.

28. Op. cit., Quest. 35, art. 2.
29. J.-L. Leuba, 'L'événement de la Parole et l'institution sacramentelle dans une théologie protestante du sacerdoce', *Recherches de sciences religieuses*, 4, 1968, p. 560.
30. *Christian Institutes*, IV, III, 16.
31. '*Ordinari vero debent ecclesiae ministri ab iis, qui iam sunt in eo gradu, quum nemo possit dare quod non habet...* The ministers of the Church must be ordained by those already in that position, because no one can give what he does not have', S. des Marets, *Collegium Theologicum*, Geneva, 1662, quoted by H. Heppe, *Die Dogmatik der evangelisch-reformierten Kirche*, Neukirchen 1958, p. 547 (S. des Marets was professor of theology at Groningen); in the same vein see L. Rimbault, *Pierre du Moulin, 1568–1658, un pasteur à l'âge classique*, Paris, 1966, p. 163.
32. J.-J. von Allmen, Op. cit., p. 50.
33. At the consecration of his son Laurent, at La Rochelle, the pastor of Charenton, Charles Drelincourt, spoke thus: 'In the name and authority of the living God, Father, Son and Holy Spirit, and in the name of the commission that has been given to me by the Lord of the province, I honour you with the charge of pastor and minister of the Holy Gospel, and give you power to preach the word of God, administer the sacraments, bless marriages and grant to repentant sinners the remission of their sins, through the infinite merits of Our Saviour Jesus Christ. In recognition of this I embrace you as my brother and recognize you as my fellow worker in the service of our great God and Saviour, to whose Grace I commend you with all the power of my soul. For a greater confirmation our brothers here will extend you their hands in association'. (C. Drelincourt, *Le saint ministère*, Charenton, 1651, pp. 175–76).
34. Canon 13.
35. *Collat.* 4, 1; quoted by J. Colson, *Les fonctions ecclésiales*, Op. cit., p. 339.
36. '*Ecclesias (Willehadus) coepit construere ac presbyteros super eas ordinare*'. Pertz, *Monumenta Hist. Germ.* II, p. 381 and 411.
37. Bull *Sacrae religionis*, of 1 February 1400; in this, Pope Boniface IX followed the opinion of the medieval canonists; but the Bishop of London asked that this permission should be withdrawn, which was done on 6 February 1403; however, the ordinations already performed remained valid.
38. Bull *Gerentes ad vos* of 16 November 1427; *Arch. Vat.*, 271, fol. 203; see J. Beyer, 'Nature et position du sacerdoce', *Nouvelle Revue Théologique*, April 1954, p. 363 ff. Pope Innocent VIII, in the Bull *Exposcit tuae devotionis* of 9 April 1489, granted the Abbot general and the four leading abbots of the Cistercian order, and their successors, the authority to ordain deacons and

sub-deacons; this was still in force in the seventeenth century.

39. On this question see L. Ott, *Grundriss der katholischen Dogmatik*, Freiburg-Basel-Vienna, 1961, p. 547: 'If it cannot be accepted that the popes in question gave way to a mistaken theological idea of their time... it must be admitted that the simple priest is an extraordinary minister of diaconal and priestly ordination, in a manner analogous to which he is an extraordinary minister of Confirmation. According to this last explanation the necessary authority to consecrate is relaxed when it is a question of the power to consecrate a priest *potestas ligata*. For it to be exercised with validity special pontifical authorization is required, whether it be by divine or ecclesiastical ordinance'. Cf. Hans Küng, *Structures de l'Eglise*, Desclée de Brouwer, Paris, 1963, pp. 245–47.

42. Classic Reformed tradition has been very rigorous on this validation of ministry by ordination. An English author of the life of Daniel Chamier, an eighteenth-century pastor, wrote of his ordination: 'Having then obtained the unanimous approval of these pastors, Daniel Chamier was solemnly authorized by the venerable pastors of Montpellier, with prayers and the laying on of hands, to fulfil the functions of an evangelical Minister, to preach God's word, administer the seals of the Covenant and oversee the discipline of God's house. Although this religious ceremony is neglected by some English independents, it is still strictly observed in all the ordinations of the continental Reformed Churches. And if any of these congregationalist preachers who had not been granted this divine, evangelical licence presumed to teach the word and administer the sacraments, the Continental Churches would summon him and have him condemned as a presumptuous and illegitimate usurper of pastoral functions'. J. Quick, *The Life of Mr Daniel Chamier*, from the translation by C. Read, *Daniel Chamier*, Paris, 1859, pp. 93–95.

43. H.J. Wotherspoon and J.M. Kirkpatrick, Op. cit., pp. 96–97.

44. Ibid., p. 98.

45. J.-J. von Allmen, Op. cit., p. 210.

46. R. Paquier, *La succession apostolique*, Eglise et Liturgie, Lusanne, 1937; E. Schlink, 'Die apostlische Sukzession', *Kerygma und Dogma*, 1961, pp. 79–114, H. Urs von Baltrasar, 'Nachfolge und Amt', *Sponsa Verbi*, Einsiedeln, 1961, pp. 80–147; A.-M. Javierre, 'Le thème de la littérature chrétienne primitive', *L'episcopat et L'Eglise universelle*, Le Cerf, Paris, 1962; Y. Congar, 'Composantes et idées de la succession', *Oecumenica*, 1966, pp. 61–80; H. Küng, *The Church*, 1967; R. Schnackenburg, 'L'apostolicité: état de recherche', *Istina*, Jan.–March, 1969, pp. 20–28.

47. P. Lebeau, 'Vatican II et l'espérance d'une Eucharistie oecuménique', *Nouvelle Revue Théologique*, Jan. 1969, pp. 23–46, makes a remarkable effort to break the deadlock.

48. There should be added the historical evidence of a presbyteral succession authorized by the popes themselves: see notes 37–39.

49. Decree *Unitatis Redintegratio*, 22, Typis polyglottis vaticanis, Rome, 1964, p. 20.

50. *Decree on ecumenism*, Typis polyglottis vaticanis, Rome, 1964, p. 21.

52. Ibid., p. 7.

53. On the idea of suppletion where there is some inadequacy, see our contribution to the book *L'intercommunion, Dialogues chrétiens*, Mame, Paris, 1970; St. Thomas Aquinas, *Summa Theologica* Suppl. Quest. 35, art. 3, suggests this idea of Christ the sovereign priest making good an accidental fault in the sacramental order: '*Summus Sacerdos suppleret defectum*'.

54. J. Daillé, *Sermons sur le Catéchisme des Eglises réformées*, Geneva, 1701, pp. 314–19.

55. On ecumenical research on ordination, cf. *La signification de l'ordination*, document d'étude de la Commission de Foi et Constitution, FO/68: 21 rev., Geneva 1968 (texte dactylographié).